Down Range

A Transitioning Veteran's Career Guide to Life's Next Phase

James D. Murphy and
William M. Duke

WILEY

CONTENTS

INTRODUCTION: YOU HAVE EVERYTHING THEY NEED

At long last, America has restarted her economic engine. Jobs are returning, revenues are growing, stock values are rising, but American business has moved past this century's first financial crisis only to face another—a crisis of leadership and values. When facing an asymmetric, constantly changing, networked marketplace, companies desperately need accountability, teamwork, and people with an ability to execute. In many ways, they need you!

Veterans have spent years—and often decades—learning how to execute as a team. We've operated under pressure, with limited information, in fluid combat scenarios. Our experience in the armed forces gave us an ability to adapt, while teaching us a process for planning and teamwork that leads to the pursuit of flawless execution. As we know, flawless execution is a pursuit, not a reality, and that mindset is what our business leaders are desperately seeking today. We may not yet possess industry vocabulary or a deep understanding of civilian business, but we have the skills modern companies need, and we can, with exceptional speed, learn to use them effectively in this new context.

Despite what too many military transition courses seem to tell us, we are not square pegs destined for a limited number of stereotyped roles. Too often, we're told we're stepping outside the wire, going into hostile territory. We must shed the fear and burden of that false mindset, and instead seize the boundless opportunity before us.

A decade ago, we were in your position, leaving the military, hearing the naysayers, and searching for a career. We soon found a home in

1

business because of—not in spite of—our years of service. Now, we work with business leaders across the country, the very people who want to hire you. These men and women regularly tell us they want accountability, and an ability to adapt, innovate, and act in an asymmetric world; they need everything you've learned as a soldier, sailor, marine, or airman. You have all the skills necessary to prosper, if not dominate, in civilian business. If you're an E-6, never let anyone say you can't be an entrepreneur. If you're an O-6, don't think people don't want to hire you because you might be perceived as high maintenance. American business needs what you have—so be proud of your background, get to work, and execute in this new world just like you did so successfully in the military. But first, you must understand a new battlespace.

Because less than one percent of Americans have served in the military, many business managers won't initially understand the values and hard skills veterans bring. They only know what they've heard or read, and that's often not accurate. You bear some of this responsibility in overcoming this gap. Selling is the lifeblood of any business, and it'll be the lifeblood of your next move because you'll be selling the most important of commodities: you. To sell yourself, you need to understand how to navigate this new battlefield, and communicate in a new vernacular so you can position yourself properly with the credibility and respect you deserve. Your job becomes showing these businessmen and women what you can offer. You've got the background and the capabilities; you have to make sure employers know it. This becomes job Number One, and we're here to help.

Nobody can predict the future, but you can design it. You've served your country, and now you deserve not just a job, but a meaningful and prosperous long-term career. That takes careful planning, and making the wrong choices at the outset can cap your potential to achieve your long-term aims. So let's start your transition with one of the first things you learned in the military: develop a plan.

This book is intended to provide career planning guidance to U.S. military veterans transitioning off active duty. Although a list of general veterans' benefits is provided in the appendices, this book is not a guide to the many resources provided by military, government, and private businesses to assist transitioning veterans. This is not a guide to getting a job. Getting a job is easy; getting one that you will enjoy, while also providing for you and your family for many years, is the true challenge that lies ahead. With this in mind, this book is a guide to developing a post-military career, not just for the first few days, weeks, or months after transitioning from active duty, but for the rest of your employed life. We will discuss how to build a successful civilian career by leveraging the skills and abilities acquired in the course of a military career.

As the authors, we are passionate about helping you and can specifically relate to your current situation. Not only are we veterans with 35 years of combined active and reserve military service in the U.S. Air Force and Navy, but our collective professional experiences include work: as a hiring manager and human resources professional in a U.S. Fortune 500 corporation; in sales and business development roles in small and large companies; as an entrepreneur and thought leader who has consulted and trained managers and executives in 30 percent of the U.S. Fortune 500 and many Global 1000 companies; and as a senior leader with command responsibilities in the military. We have also created a highly acclaimed career-planning seminar for U.S. Army transitioning veterans. Our perspective is unique. We have experienced the challenges that veterans face as they transition to civilian careers from every perspective: that of veterans without a clear career path; employers; highly active members of the military reserve force; corporate trainers; and employees in large for-profit corporations, a mid-size not-for-profit corporation, and a small for-profit company. As consultants, we have been inside the walls of companies in many different industries, witnessed the challenges modern businesses face, and recognized the great value and skills that veterans possess to meet those challenges.

This book follows a proven career-planning process, one born of military planning principles that we at Afterburner Inc., our training and consulting firm, have been teaching to business executives all over the world since 1996. The effectiveness and popularity of that planning process is due, in part, to the principles of planning commonly practiced in all the military services. These are skills that veterans possess and businesses need. This book will help you tap those principles to develop a career and to demonstrate your value to potential employers.

It All Starts with a Plan

One of the most significant skills that you possess, even if your military experience is as a junior enlisted soldier, sailor, marine, or airman, is your ability to plan.

In this book we apply the fundamentals of planning to achieve a set of career objectives. To do that, we need to introduce some greater detail about the six-step planning process that we will be utilizing for the rest of this book. The flawless execution planning process proceeds through the following steps:

STEP 1: Determine the objective.

STEP 2: Identify the threats (or challenges) to accomplishing the objective.

STEP 3: Determine the resources available or needed to achieve the objective.

STEP 4: Evaluate lessons learned.

STEP 5: Determine the course of action.

STEP 6: Plan for contingencies.

This book provides a structure for defining, planning, and achieving your career objective. We will, as we proceed through each step in the planning process, provide guidance, recommendations, considerations, new knowledge, and lessons learned that will help inform your planning. We will address the many common threats and resources that you need to consider that will inform the actions you will need to take to achieve your career objectives. We will help you develop your own personal value proposition that will enable you to sell your skills and abilities to any perspective employer. We will provide guidance on interview preparation and conduct, and address how to leverage social networking as a highly valuable resource in your career development. Perhaps most important of all, we will show you how to create a clear and measurable career high-definition destination (HDD) that will act as the driving force behind achieving the career that is right for you.

But, first, you need to prepare yourself mentally for your transition. You need to change your mindset. In the first chapter, we will help you do that.

Let's begin!

CHAPTER 1

TRANSITION YOUR MINDSET: IT'S A BRAND NEW MISSION

Who are the most influential people in your particular military community? Is it the chief of staff of your respective service or the leader of your military branch or community? Perhaps you closely follow the activities, blogs, broadcasts, or other messages of the senior enlisted member of your service, such as the sergeant major of the army or marine corps. These are individuals who you would recognize instantly if you were to meet them, but would you recognize a similar leader in the business world? Be honest with yourself. Can you name a single chief executive officer (CEO) from any one of the U.S. Fortune 500 companies?

If Jack Welch and Steve Jobs are the only names that come to mind, you need to develop a little more knowledge of *current* business topics. (Jack Welch is retired and Steve Jobs, sadly, passed away in 2011.) If neither of these names is familiar to you, and you can't at least recall what companies they led, then put this book down now, go to the Internet, and do a simple search to find out who, exactly, they are. You lack the most basic knowledge of business history. We could tell you who those two people are in this paragraph, but then we would be failing to communicate something far more important, which is that you must be committed to learning about this new world you are about to enter. You must be willing to research information related to every potential employer so that you are able to both answer and

7

ask interview questions in an intelligent way that convinces a potential employer that you are a good fit for their company.

Take a look at the picture below (Figure 1.1). Do you recognize this person? Do you know the company that he is associated with?

If you do not recognize this person, know his name, or have any idea what company he leads, you are not the exception. In our veteran transition seminars less than 5 percent recognize this person, and, of those, we could count on one hand the number of individuals who could tell us this person's name.

His name is Jeff Bezos. If you are still thinking, "So what if I've never heard of him?" you're not alone. But his face has been on the cover of countless magazines since the last millennium! He was *Time* magazine's Man of the Year in 1999 and *Forbes* magazine's Business Person of the Year for 2012. He has been in the global spotlight for well over a decade.

Still not sure what company he runs? Jeff Bezos is the founder and CEO of Amazon.com, the world's largest online retailer.

We chose Mr. Bezos as an introductory brain teaser for a number of reasons. He's one of the most influential and famous business leaders

Figure 1.1   Joe Klamar/AFP/Getty Images

in the United States today. We also chose him because his company, Amazon, is one of the most disruptive influences in the retail market today. Great companies that are as different from each other as Barnes and Noble Booksellers and the consumer electronics giant Best Buy are struggling mightily with the massive negative impact that Amazon has had upon their businesses. If your career takes you into the retail industry, you may find yourself struggling against the powerful changes wrought by Mr. Bezos's Amazon. If you are a consumer—and we all are—then you probably already recognize that Amazon can often provide a cheaper product and deliver it directly to your door.

There is one more important fact about Mr. Bezos and his company that we must point out. Amazon is one of the top employers of veterans. In 2011, 25 percent of Amazon's new hires at its fulfillment centers were veterans. That led *G.I. Jobs* magazine to rank Amazon at the top of its list of military-friendly employers. Amazon recognizes the outstanding skill sets that military veterans bring, particularly in its highly logistics-oriented business.

The opportunities are out there in the civilian world, waiting for you, and there are many of them. But to take advantage of them, first you need to get grounded in the differences between the military world you are leaving and the world of business you may be entering. You need to develop some basic understanding of how these two worlds are different.

Unfortunately, the military and civilian worlds often misunderstand each other. Some civilians have a limited comprehension of military service; servicemen and women often misunderstand the significant drivers of a business and assume, incorrectly, that the day-to-day activities of civilian employment are very much like that of non-combat-oriented military service. Some civilians may have some anxiety about hiring veterans because they perceive military service as being solely about discipline and taking orders, and they wonder how veterans will function outside a task-oriented rank structure. Both sides misunderstand the real differences between business and military service. Transitioning veterans must help potential employers see beyond misconceptions while carefully addressing the differences that really matter.

In the military, we worry about budgets and committing our allocated funds before the end of the fiscal year. In business, we worry about sales pipelines and cash flow. In the military, we worry about national security—a self-sacrificing responsibility that far exceeds our unit or service as a whole. Many businesses worry about keeping proprietary or sensitive data safe. Servicemen and women are bound by oath and law to high ideals, whereas businesses are bound to shareholders. Corporations exist to increase stockholder value, and often, profits and civic good can go hand-in-hand. Businesses are not necessarily evil empires; their profits can enable the dreams of their employees and shareholders. If businesses are led and managed well, they can grow and thrive for many decades while contributing to the overall welfare of their employees, customers, communities, nation, and even the world. As a veteran, do not forget that the military exists in part so that civilians can engage in free commerce and the pursuit of life, liberty, and happiness.

Few companies live very long, however. The average company goes out of business within five years. Some of the largest corporations in the world are still quite young. Consider that you have served in a military that has existed since the founding of this country in 1776. Consider also that the largest company in the United States, Wal-Mart, with a number of employees that is comparable to all the uniformed servicemen and women in the U.S. military services combined, was started in 1962, a mere 51 years ago. Apple is 37 years old; Google is less than 20, and Twitter is less than 10. As these companies have risen, others have become obsolete or fallen to acquisitions or bankruptcies. Business landscapes can change almost as rapidly as a battlefield.

Serving in the military and working in the civilian sector share some important common points, but also have differences you should understand as you begin your transition. First, let's consider the most important similarities. All organizations, whether military or business, require a multitude of skills for you to survive in their environment; great organizations, however, master a set of six principles that should be very familiar to you by virtue of your military experience and training. Those principles are leadership, organization, communication, knowledge, experience, and discipline. We call these the LOCKED on Teams principles of high performance. We will address these principles in more detail in Chapter 2. We introduce them now to emphasize that these are the very skills that companies need. You have them … you just have to help potential employers understand your skills and recognize them in their own unique business context. Doing so will help you land that first job that is a good fit for you and a great step toward achieving a long and prosperous civilian career.

SCALE AND VARIETY

As you transition from active duty service to a civilian career, you are leaving an enormous organization that employs 1.5 million active duty and 850,000 reserve personnel. That makes the sum of soldiers, sailors, marines, and airmen larger than the largest employer in the world, Wal-Mart, which employs 2.2 million people worldwide. The U.S. military organization has been around for more than two centuries. Arguably, no other employment system is more mature, comprehensive, and complicated than the bureaucracy that maintains our armed forces.

Because of its unique nature and purpose, the military is highly protective of its servicemen and women. In civilian business, you may not find that same level of care, protection, and interest as you did in the military. You may be thinking, "Yeah, but the military sent me into combat!" True, the military will endanger your life like few civilian businesses can. But it will care for your personal welfare outside of the inherent dangers of service better than most any other company. By contrast, a civilian employer will likely take care to keep you physically safe, but may show less concern for your personal welfare. Some companies will rival, if not exceed, the military in the benefits they provide. The point is that companies vary widely and it will be up to you to weigh the strengths and weaknesses of each to suit your needs. You are about to enter a wilderness of employment possibilities, each with its own values, rules, processes, and procedures.

There are more than 27 million licensed businesses in the United States, and every single one has its own way of doing business. Of course, 6 million of those companies have a single employee: the owner. Most veterans will not choose to work in companies with less than five employees (although those opportunities are not without merit), and will look instead to work in larger, more stable companies. In that case, career-seekers can consider that their actual range of potential employers includes 500,000 different companies that employ 20 to 100 people each. There are around 1,000 businesses in the United States that employ more than 10,000 people. There are millions of different companies that might hire you, and they each have a different purpose, a different way of managing people, and different opportunities.

This book will help you navigate the wilderness of variety, but you must apply what you read in these pages to each unique employment context with good judgment and careful research.

HIERARCHY VERSUS FLATNESS

In the military, you lived and worked in a hierarchical culture with two primary classifications, officer and enlisted, that roughly correspond to the management and labor or worker classifications in civilian business. In the military, there are varying enlisted and commissioned ranks and a defined set of rules and customs that govern the system. Everyone knows exactly where and how they fit. Rank insignia can easily indicate who is in charge. Civilian business is quite different.

Modern businesses tend to have fewer levels of grade, rank, or positional authority. For instance, in an operations center in a 100-person business, much like what one might call a military TOC or an OPCON, you might find 90 employees in two or three positional grades and a management staff of about 10 in two or three positional grades for a total of four to six grades or ranks. If that same center were a military operation, one would easily find at least a dozen different ranks or grades working side by side. This is part of what we mean when we say that civilian businesses are *flat*, compared to the military

workplace. It also means that the chain of command is much less strat-
ified. Consider the number of individuals in the chain of command
between an E-1 recruit and the president of the United States. In some
of the largest Fortune 500 companies, there may be no more than five
people in the chain of command between a newly hired, entry-level
worker and the chief executive officer (CEO) at the very top of the
organization.

Although all companies have hierarchies, they often vary in their
functions and trappings. Particularly in more modern times, CEOs
often don't sit in oak-paneled offices with expensive paintings on the
walls. Many don't wear expensive suits, and instead dress down, rarely
wearing a tie. Many corporate leaders sit in private cubicles or open
offices, and instead of addressing a leader as sir or ma'am, many civilian employees call their supervisors by their first names. In general, the
workplace has become a first-name-basis, informal environment. You
will probably have to shed your rigid military courtesies and adapt to
that informal environment.

The tendency toward flatness and informality in businesses is, in
itself, not a significant issue for you. You are transitioning into an
environment where no one wears a uniform with their rank sewn on
their collar or sleeve, and you may find yourself in a matrixed organization that has an ambiguous chain of command. You may report to
several individuals at once. In matrixed companies, you may also find
yourself assigned periodically to various ad hoc teams assembled from
different departments and divisions. Those teams may have no clear
chain of command or appointed leader. Companies have learned that
a matrixed organization can provide greater agility and efficiency;
however, it also creates greater ambiguity of accountability. Matrixed
ad hoc teams often suffer from poor execution due to a lack of leadership and organization, and, in these cases your skills to *get the job done*
will shine. Even if you are not formally appointed as the leader of such
a team, you have the skills and abilities to lead it—you just have to
apply those skills in a soft and diplomatic way rather than *pulling rank*.

The bottom line for you is that you shouldn't expect a great
deal of personal mentoring or task-oriented direction in a business

environment. You will be expected to do your job, particularly if you are in a skilled, professional, or management position, without much supervision.

MISSION-DRIVEN VERSUS PROFIT-DRIVEN

The military exists to defend our country and it subsists upon an enormous budget that provides for training and operational commitments. Businesses exist to provide products and services to their customers and to return profits to shareholders. The profits those businesses make are taxed to provide the budgetary resources needed to staff, equip, and train military forces. The military depends upon the profitability of businesses for its continued survival, while businesses depend upon the peace and protection that the military provides. We all benefit from this cooperative relationship.

Although the relationship appears simple and the purpose direct, the differences in mission and purpose provide a stark fiscal contrast between military and business worlds. Military forces spend money while businesses make it. In your military experience, you probably enjoyed a fiscal environment that was more-or-less fixed. You had an annual budget and you had to spend it all by the end of the fiscal year. Those resources were tightly controlled and overseen. In a business, your budget may change throughout the course of the year, largely depending on the cash flow of the company. In general, budgets change very slowly in the military. In businesses, budget resources may change very rapidly in response to market fluctuations and competitive forces; they can change overnight, and frequently do. And, in some businesses, varying cash flow may drive very short-term budgets.

As you transition into business you must recognize that you are expected to be a good steward of fiscal resources, just like you were in the military. Some of you, however, may find yourselves in a position where you have a compelling need to drive revenue, especially if you are in the business development, marketing, or sales divisions of a company. We all agree that, in a military context, the waste of life, whether in combat or training, is a very serious issue; in business, that same level of seriousness must be accorded to the waste of money or the failure to generate profit. In business, cash is vital.

SERVICE VERSUS EMPLOYMENT

We call it *the service* for a reason. We were called, for one reason or another, to put our country and fellow servicemembers' welfare before our own. We swore an oath that required us to obey laws that do not bind our fellow citizens. Consequently, we are not free to walk away from our service commitments or enlistment contract without permission, but that commitment is not a one-way obligation. The service branch or the country as a whole is obligated to care for you in ways that far exceed the care given by most companies. We hope that you are aware of the full spectrum of veterans' benefits that are available to you. (Refer to Appendix K.)

Whether you signed an enlistment contract or earned a commission at the beginning of your military career, you were obligated to serve for a period of several years. Once you took that oath, you couldn't just walk away. As a civilian employee, you have no such commitment. You can quit whenever you want and for whatever reason (of course, a company can always let you go, as well). Leaving a job may not be the best career decision, but no one can stop you.

Be aware that many laws govern civilian employment, and these laws vary by state, while company policies will vary within those laws. In general, however, a company is not free to terminate your employment without due process. For instance, in the military, you can't be discharged before the end of your contract without due process whether through an administrative separation or a force-wide reduction that addresses a specific population and category of service-members. Civilian employment law is very similar. In some states, companies can't fire you without a reason, whether that reason is based upon individual performance, the decision to eliminate a job classification, or the choice to lay off employees in response to diminishing profits. However—and this is a big *however*—most companies have policies that are supported by law allowing them to classify new employees as having been hired into a *probationary period*. A probationary period is usually the first 60 to 90 days of employment in a new company. During that period, a company can terminate employment without explanation. When starting any job, do your best and be dedicated to success. Meet and exceed the expectations of a new employer for the first few months of your employment. Do a good job and you won't become a victim of the probationary period. After that period, keep doing a good job, develop your career, and become familiar with your employer's policies and the state laws that govern your employment.

INTRUSION VERSUS PRIVACY

Military service means subjecting yourself to an extreme level of intrusiveness. You may have had full background investigations to maintain a security clearance and annual medical assessments or physical examinations. Perhaps you have been assisted by your superiors as you handled very personal issues. You have had general military training on an annual basis about your personal finances, substance abuse, suicide indicators, stress management, and much more. You have lived side by side with peers, subordinates, and superiors and shared the same messing, bathing, and restroom facilities. You have been subjected to drug testing on demand. Personal property stored in government facilities where you live or work is subject to inspection at any time. You must conform to physical standards that prohibit obesity and, failing those standards, you can be forced onto a physical and dietary regimen. In short, you have not enjoyed the many freedoms you have sworn to protect; but you have enjoyed being part of a service that has cared deeply and intrusively about you and tried to protect and nurture you as a highly valued asset.

Frankly, military service can be highly discriminatory from a civilian perspective. The special demands and context of military service have required, as one U.S. Army general called it, "intrusive leadership." If you become obese, the military will terminate your service. If you are female, there are still a few occupations within the services that prohibit your involvement. There are a host of manageable physical conditions that prohibit many Americans from serving in uniform. (Too old? Sorry, you can't serve.) But, this is not so in the world of civilian employment. Unlike military service, laws prohibit businesses from discriminating against anyone based upon sex, weight, or age. In fact, the law prohibits companies from discriminating against those with physical disabilities, and requires businesses to make reasonable accommodations to employ disabled employees who are otherwise qualified to execute the requirements of a specific job.

Your civilian employer, predominately because of the legal restrictions, is likely to appear far less interested in your personal welfare. They are prevented from asking questions of you such as: How old are you? Are you married? Do you have children? Employers are also not allowed to ask many other questions during the application process such as race, sex, religious preference, and such because they are closely scrutinized under equal opportunity requirements. In addition, employers are subject to a host of other laws that hold them liable for injuries, accidents, and other damages or influences. Although you were safety conscious in your military career, you didn't worry too much about many of the liabilities and legal boundaries between you and other servicemembers. You just did what you needed to do to get the job done and take care of people. Outside the military, you may encounter a very different attitude, one often driven by fear of legal retribution, toward you and your life and activities outside of the workplace. Civilian businesses are very unintrusive in comparison to military life.

CONSTANT DUTY VERSUS ON THE CLOCK

Generally, however, your civilian career won't demand you be ready and able 24 hours a day, seven days a week as your military service can. Laws require employers to offer breaks and compensating pay for work performed beyond regular hours. In other words, you are protected from a forced overseas deployment where you will work 18 or 20 hours per day for months on end without relief.

In your military service, you are a salaried employee regardless of your status as enlisted or officer. In your new civilian career, you may not be salaried. Instead, you may punch in and out to a time clock or work based upon a part-time contract. If you do become a salaried employee, you should expect to work more than 40 hours per week; however, you may be expected to maintain focus on your responsibilities 24 hours a day, as you did in your military duties. The boss may call you at home, and you will very likely take work home on a regular basis unless you spend extra hours at the office—and e-mail knows no boundaries. If you are an hourly employee, you may be encouraged to work additional hours, but if you do, you will be entitled to additional pay.

Life in business may be a significantly different cultural experience for you. But, in most ways, it provides a greater quality of life than you are used to, so long as you remain employed in a career that you enjoy and receive adequate compensation. Your business future can also provide an unlimited opportunity to take you as high and far in both compensation and life experiences as you and your family can imagine.

You are about to enter a new world. This world has already touched your life, but your focus has not been directed toward it. You must now change your focus. You must educate yourself about this new world of employment.

LEARNING THE LANGUAGE

Do you know what *EBITDA* means? We won't make you look this one up. We'll tell you that it means *earnings before interest, taxation, depreciation, and amortization.* Not helpful? Why on earth would we mention such a thing? When we discussed the differences between military service and civilian employment, we indicated that businesses are concerned with money or cash flow. EBITDA is one of the principal financial concepts that businesses use to measure the all-important bottom line. In some ways, EBITDA is a measure of vitality like a human being's heart rate and blood pressure. Do you need to know what EBITDA means? That is not an easy question to answer. You might. Many companies utilize EBITDA to measure performance and include it on a balanced scorecard. If you plan to obtain a management position, you may be graded on a balanced scorecard that determines your annual performance review (evaluation, fitness report, and so on). You may be in a position in which the EBITDA determines how much you receive in bonuses. It can mean real money to you!

After five years of commissioned service as a U.S. Army Ranger in the 82nd Airborne, young Robert McDonald left the service to pursue a business career in 1980. From July 2007 until May 2013, McDonald served as the CEO of a Fortune 50 business with $85 billion in revenues. That company, Procter & Gamble (P&G) manufactures iconic brands found in any general merchandise store in America. P&G's brands include Tide, Old Spice, Crest, Oil of Olay, Pampers, Gillette, Bounty, Pepto Bismol, Duracell, Bounce, Pert, Downey, and Mr. Clean.

Another veteran, Jim Skinner, served nearly 10 years as an enlisted petty officer in the U.S. Navy. He never earned a college degree, but became CEO of McDonald's.

These veterans didn't know any more than you about manufacturing consumer goods or running fast food restaurants when they left active duty. But, what they learned in military service prepared them well for their success in business. Those same lessons and military values will serve you well, regardless of the positions you pursue or attain.

We wrote this book, not to give you a crash course in business, but to help guide you through your transition. We cannot begin to address the vast business knowledge you'd need to know for the myriad career options before you, but because we live in the age of accessible information, much of what you need to know is available online and through networks of friends, colleagues, mentors, and associations. In the following chapters, we will guide you to resources and help you develop and utilize these networks.

Before you read further, consider the following question: Do you want someone or some company to give you a job, or do you want to develop and direct your own career? If you just want a job, there are plenty out there. They probably won't be jobs that you enjoy, are proud to perform, or derive the necessary economic benefits to support yourself and your family. If, on the other hand, you are interested in taking charge of your career, and building one that will satisfy all your needs, read further.

CHAPTER DEBRIEF

- You must focus your attention to learning about the environment you are about to enter, researching every potential employment opportunity while you continuously develop an understanding of this new environment.
- The variety of civilian employment options are, for all practical purposes, virtually infinite, with cultures and processes that vary widely from company to company.
- The hierarchies within civilian companies are generally flat with a comparatively informal chain of command and often ambiguous reporting relationships.
- Civilian companies are predominately profit-driven. Even non-profit organizations must take extreme care with their cash flow.
- Unlike military service, laws prevent or discourage companies from intrusion into your private life.

CHAPTER 2

TRANSLATING THE VALUES YOU BRING TO BUSINESS

Some years ago, you heard the call to serve your country, and you answered. However, as you complete your military service, you're answering a new call. America needs your talent in business so our economy can remain as strong as our military, and so our private industry can continue to fund the budgets our nation's freedom requires. Now, you generally won't find recruiting posters for corporate jobs, but companies do want you. They are realizing that the skills that veterans have are the very skills that built the U.S. economy after World War II. Veterans led the post-war boom that made modern America into the world's dominant economy.

With only about 1 percent of modern Americans having ever served in the military, our generation of veterans is much smaller than the World War II generation, of whom there were sixteen million, representing 33 percent of the male population over age fifteen. The valuable skills that military service provides are becoming an increasingly rare commodity for employers, and those skill sets are more valuable than ever before. Among them, one of the most valuable is leadership.

Businesses are beginning to recognize the leadership qualities veterans exhibit. In just the past few years, business magazines such as the *Harvard Business Review* and *Fortune* have showcased how the front-line leaders in the wars in Afghanistan and Iraq have produced the leadership qualities that businesses need to remain competitive in the modern environment. They've learned that frontline leaders can navigate teams through fast-paced, dangerous environments to accomplish a mission with little guidance and in the face of great ambiguity and uncertainty—the very same type of environment that businesses often face. Veterans know how to execute under rapidly changing and often treacherous circumstances.

In today's business environments, every good leader is concerned about how well his or her organization executes and adapts to change. Execution has been on the list of top concerns of CEOs for years now, but the turbulence of the past few years underscores the necessity for adaptability and execution to survive and prosper in the new economy.

What's the secret to executing and propelling an organization to the next level? We believe it's infusing an organization with military experience. A growing body of evidence demonstrates the positive results generated by the experiences of military veterans.

In 2006, Korn/Ferry International, in cooperation with the Economist Intelligence Unit, published an astonishing report that illustrated the extraordinary value of military leadership experience in the private sector. The report, "Military Experience & CEOs: Is There a Link?" demonstrates unequivocally that there is indeed a connection between business success and military leadership experience.[1] The report showed that S&P 500 CEOs, as a demographic group, are nearly three times more likely to have served in one of the four U.S. military services than the general population of U.S. adult males. It also showed that companies led by these former military leaders outperformed, on average, other S&P 500 firms. These CEOs also lasted longer in their positions by nearly three years on average, so, not only did these leaders perform better, they were more committed to their companies over the long haul. These leaders could translate strategy into action, an imperative skill in today's environment.

The ability to make decisions and act when faced with new challenges and limited information is a key skill possessed by veterans.

---

[1] Korn/Ferry International. "Military Experience & CEOs: Is There a Link?," 2006.

Whether you flew military aircraft, navigated ships, or led troops in Afghanistan or Iraq, your daily life depended upon solving problems and executing your decisions in a rapidly changing environment. Business leaders need those same skills.

Every business in America can benefit from the experience gained by leaders in the U.S. military. In light of the current economic turmoil and the proven capacity of military leaders to execute and excel in unstable business environments, companies need your talents. You possess abilities to plan, set goals, communicate, and motivate others that no business school can teach. You have practiced and honed your decision-making skills in life-and-death situations. Companies that stake a claim on you, a rare commodity, and actively recruit you will certainly position themselves to execute in the turbulent future ahead—but you must know how to articulate the assets you bring.

One of the reasons that you are so valuable is that there is an inevitable dearth of leaders, growing worse year after year. We have a baby-boom generation that has been leading companies for many years, but these experienced leaders are retiring in droves. Our generation of warriors is too few to fill their shoes. There is a leadership deficit on the horizon and companies are preparing for it. Your challenge as a veteran is to translate your experience into the very leadership qualities that employers need.

Have you ever heard the term *GenFluxer*? A GenFluxer is short for a member of "Generation Flux," which is a term coined by Robert Safian, the editor of *Fast Company* magazine. The term expresses how young leaders in many cutting-edge companies are leading and succeeding in extremely turbulent environments. There are many very young CEOs who are harnessing the chaos of the markets and leading very successfully in that environment. Perhaps the poster child of the GenFluxers is Mark Zuckerberg of Facebook. Interestingly, though, Safian considers the former ISAF commander of the U.S. forces in Afghanistan, General Stanley McChrystal, to be a sort of mentor to GenFluxers. Safian writes:

> In today's chaos, leadership is more critical than ever—but a different kind of leadership. There is no single model of what it will take to succeed now. But

drawing on examples from many different kinds of organizations—including the
U.S. Army, ... we can begin to define the qualities of successful GenFlux leaders.[2]

Safian and many others are speaking out on behalf of you and the
value you bring to employers. You just have to take advantage of the
groundswell of support.

The greatest challenge you may face is translating your leadership
skills into a language that employers can understand. Except in the
few uncommon instances in which a potential employer is a veteran,
hiring managers don't understand military terminology, and, unfortunately, those potential employers that do understand a military resume
will probably never see it if you apply for the job electronically. With
an enormous volume of applicants for every posted job, companies
have resorted to utilizing digital applicant tracking systems (ATSs).
The ATS software scans for key words to match to a job description.
So, if you are not using the right language, you're less likely to be
matched to a particular job, regardless of your level of qualification.
Automated systems are one of the greatest threats to your success in
receiving a job offer. We will address the particulars of how to defeat
the ATS threat later. For now, let's focus on translating your skills and
experiences into assets employers will understand and value.

LOCKED

As a military veteran, you bring several unique qualities to any
potential employer, qualities that distinguish you from your civilian
peers. You bring experience in leadership, organization, communication, knowledge management, battlefield operations, and discipline.
To keep our affinity to our military roots intact, we've developed
the acronym LOCKED: leadership, organization, communication,
knowledge, experience, and discipline.

Leadership deals with developing the team, aligning it toward the
objective, and holding the individual members accountable for their

---

[2]Safian, Robert. "Secrets of the Flux Leader," *Fast Company* magazine, November
2012, p. 101.

commitments and responsibilities. Organization refers to defining the roles of all the team members and identifying the relevant processes and documents necessary to guide the team. Communication refers to the sharing, coordinating, and dissemination of relevant information. The next two characteristics, knowledge and experience, are closely related but not the same. Knowledge is the *know what*, and experience is the *know how*. Knowledge deals with acquisition, identification, and utilization of information, whereas battlefield experience helps bridge the gap between the known and the unknown; you know how to execute, even with imperfect information. Finally, discipline is about focusing the team on the right things and keeping progress on track.

Let's look at each category in a bit more detail. What follows is a brief overview of the qualities and activities that high-performing teams and their leaders exhibit. As you read through each, consider what skills you have developed in your military career that relate to each category.

Leadership

Military leaders understand the importance of taking responsibility for mission accomplishment, a quality often less common in the business world, where flat organizations and ad hoc collaborative teams contribute to a dispersion of responsibility among a faceless *them*. Furthermore, some civilian managers are less adept at holding their subordinates responsible; sometimes policies or structures prevent them from doing so. Military leaders understand that authority may be delegated, but not responsibility. Leaders are constantly updating where they are and where they are going to increase situational awareness for themselves and their team.

Veterans also lead by example. They follow their own rules and view ethics as the foundation of their decision making. They not only listen to their subordinates, but they also actively seek their opinions and respond positively to constructive criticism. They treasure those who follow them for their contributions, and actively engage in their development, because someday those subordinates will take their place. Leadership means:

- Leading by example.
- Holding yourself and others accountable.
- Reinforcing standards and established processes.
- Cultivating situational awareness.
- Facilitating collaboration.
- Empowering, developing, and engaging subordinates.

Organization

Veterans recognize the importance of standards, develop them when needed, and enforce them. Former military personnel are not only organized in a physical sense, but also in the way they think and solve problems. They plan according to an organized process; they communicate in an organized manner; they execute in a rhythmic, coordinated fashion; and they learn from mistakes and successes through a rigorous methodology (e.g., after-action reviews and debriefings). Veterans understand the value of habit and its role in effective execution. Organization means:

- Establishment of clear goals, measurements, and roles.
- Management of plans and projects.
- Quality management and control.
- Process and continuous improvement.
- Workflow analysis and management.
- Time management.

Communication

Veterans communicate with clarity, in spoken words and in writing. They understand the need to link today's activities with a strategy and a planned outcome. They arrange information in a coherent manner, and brief it to others to achieve high levels of comprehension. Communication means:

- Verbal and non-verbal communication and writing skills.
- Customer service.

- Conducting formal briefings and presentations.
- Reinforcing and aligning tactical, strategic, and organizational goals and objectives.

Knowledge and Experience

Veterans are not only well educated in the technical requirements of their areas of responsibility, but also in the limits of knowledge in ambiguous or changing circumstances. They are not paralyzed by insufficient information; they act. And, in so doing, they learn rapidly from their mistakes to improve and adapt. They incorporate a variety of opinions and experiences in planning and decision making, and train to close gaps in understanding and experience, while subjecting their plans to assessment and critique by others. Knowledge and experience means:

- Knowledge.
- Formal education.
- Professional certification.
- Organizational learning competencies.
- Teaching, training, and facilitation.
- Experience.
- Broad scope and responsibilities of positions held.
- Demonstration of ability to utilize knowledge to drive results.

Discipline

Veterans are not only disciplined to follow orders and adhere to rigorous standards, but they also are self-disciplined. They are able to focus intently upon their objective, prioritize activities, and hold the interests of their assigned objective and their team above their own self-interests without task-saturating their teams. They consider risk as a component of the planning process. Discipline means:

- Managing stress and task saturation.
- Executing responsibilities in high-risk environments.

- Mission and others before self.
- Focus on objectives.
- Delivering on commitments.

With these qualities—these assets—in mind, you can begin crafting your own individualized *value proposition* and planning to answer potential interview questions. As we move to the first step in career planning, you can incorporate many of the talent sets that you may not have realized you possess.

Your objective is to create your own unique recruiting poster in the form of a resume, a value proposition, and a virtual signature that points a finger directly at an employer and calmly, but sternly says, "You want me."

CHAPTER DEBRIEF

- The current business environment is one of turbulence and ambiguity that requires leadership to execute and adapt to complexity. This business environment requires the same valuable skill sets that veterans of the wars of the past 12 years have developed.
- These skill sets are hard to find as the baby-boom generation rapidly exits the workforce and younger generations have significantly less leadership experience to fill the void.
- Business leaders and management scholars have begun to recognize the valuable skill sets veterans possess, and have begun to communicate that value.
- The LOCKED model of high-performing teams is the model that concisely structures the varied skill sets that veterans possess.
- Translating one's individual skills and experiences into a language that employers can understand is one of the most critical activities for veterans to perform.

YES, THEY NEED YOUR SKILLS

In your time in the military, you may have acquired a set of skills that have direct equivalency in the business world. You may have earned a bachelor's or even an advanced degree that is relevant in either the military or civilian professions, but there are certain skills you have developed that are rare in the business world. These are the skills that employers are finally recognizing. Here is what some experts are saying:

> Veterans reentering the civilian workforce are increasingly finding a warm welcome. That's especially true for young officers who have led combat units on the front lines. According to headhunters, human resources executives, and business school admissions officers, these candidates—most in their late 20s or early 30s, with a college degree and leadership experience far beyond that of their civilian peers—are stars waiting to happen.
>
> **—Brian O'Keefe, "Battle-Tested: How a Decade of War Has Created A New Generation of Elite Business Leaders."** *Fortune.* **March 22, 2010.**

> Military work is risky, pressured, and fast-changing. It calls for seemingly contradictory capabilities: absolute clarity about the mission at a high level, extraordinary adaptability on the ground, and a knack for managing complex, technically precise systems. These are the same skills that companies today need to prevail in a climate of intense economic uncertainty.
>
> **—"Leadership Lessons From the Military"** *Harvard Business Review.* **November 2010.**

> The returning veterans are bringing skills that seem to be on the wane in American society, qualities we really need now: crisp decision making, rigor, optimism, entrepreneurial creativity, a larger sense of purpose and real patriotism.
>
> **—Joe Klein, "The New Greatest Generation."** *Time.* **August 29, 2011.**

(continued)

(continued)

Dealing with ambiguity, that's something that I think the military is quite good at.

—Jeffrey Immelt, CEO, General Electric, quoted by Brian O'Keefe in "Battle-Tested: How a Decade of War Has Created A New Generation of Elite Business Leaders." *Fortune.* **March 22, 2010.**

Let's be clear: hiring a veteran can be one of the best decisions any of us can make. These are leaders with discipline, training and a passion for service.

—William S. Simon, CEO, Wal-Mart U.S., quoted by Brian O'Keefe in "Battle-Tested: How a Decade of War Has Created A New Generation of Elite Business Leaders." *Fortune.* **March 22, 2010.**

CHAPTER 3

BEFORE YOU STEP OUTSIDE THE WIRE, DETERMINE YOUR OBJECTIVE

THE SIX STEPS OF PLANNING

1. **Determine the mission objective**.
2. Identify the threats.
3. Identify your resources.
4. Evaluate lessons learned.
5. Develop a course of action.
6. Plan for contingencies.

Planning is serious business. Without good planning, execution toward an objective becomes much more difficult. Even though managers in business know this well, they often fail to plan effectively. Business leaders often conceive of an idea or objective, and then act to execute it without the planning so familiar to veterans. Too often, an excited team begins a project, becomes overwhelmed by the minor tactical issues that they encounter along the way, and ultimately falls short of achieving their goal. Sometimes, they become lost in a flurry of insignificant activity. That activity makes them feel good because they are doing something; they are busy. But, doing *something* rather than the *right* thing just wastes time and energy.

The Nike slogan "Just Do It" isn't a sufficient driver of success in businesses any more than it is in military endeavors. As veterans, we know that every great plan starts with an objective. At a tactical level, we understand that a good objective is stated clearly to eliminate ambiguity. We also know that a good objective is measureable in an indisputably quantifiable way. You are either successful or you are not; there is no question about which it was. Good objectives are also achievable. Military teams avoid risky missions with a low chance of success, but too many business project teams fail to begin with clear, measurable, and achievable objectives—and this is where your experience can help. The proper statement of a tactical objective is where success begins.

If you don't know where you are going, how do you expect to get where you want to go? Do you have a career objective? Does that objective look something like "I will have X job on X date." If you could simply fill in these two X's in this simple statement of objective, would that compel you to take deliberate and well-considered action toward achieving it? Our belief is that the answer for you, and everyone else, is no. Too many people get confused between an objective and a set of long-range goals.

We believe that there are three types of goals. Tactical goals are very short in range and objective. The successful execution of many tactical goals are required in order to achieve the next level of goal, which we call strategic intent. By consistently focusing on what you intend to achieve rather than what you can objectively measure in a tactical objective, you are better able to direct and adapt the tactical efforts.

A strategy, though, is not an ultimate objective. A strategy is simply a clever means of achieving that long-range objective or future state. Strategies focus our daily tactics, which ultimately lead us to our long-range goals. Those strategies must adapt and change over the years as we learn new things about the environment, and while we affect and change that environment through our own efforts. Remember what the Prussian military planner Helmuth von Moltke once said: "No plan survives first contact with the enemy."[1]

---

[1] von Moltke, Helmuth. *Militarisch Werke*, vol. 2.

What do we call that ultimate objective? We call long-range objectives a high-definition destination, or HDD. The science of planning requires that we have a detailed or high-definition description of the future we wish to create. Our strategy informs us of the primary means by which we will accomplish the HDD. From each strategic intended effect, we determine the tactics needed to achieve it. This three-tiered planning model is what we teach and facilitate with our clients. It works for individuals, teams, and organizations. We have used this model to set direction with the senior leaders of billion-dollar corporations as well as the career aspirations of individuals. A good planning model is a good planning model regardless of the scale and application.

For you and your career HDD, there are many different ways to describe success. The more detail you put into describing your future, the easier it will be to identify the strategy and tactics you must pursue to achieve it. Your career is one of the most significant aspects of your life, now and in the future. Have you considered how it all fits together?

The HDD is where your career starts; it's the most important career-planning exercise you'll ever do. It will inform the strategy you must pursue to be successful, which, in turn, will inform the day-to-day tactics that you employ. Your career HDD is not a description of a job that you plan to start the first day after you transition from active duty service. Instead, it is the description of your professional life 5, 10, or even 20 years in the future. Your career HDD is the description of your life if you were to jump in a time machine and travel to some future date, open your eyes, and describe the future you see. It's very different from saying, "I will have X job on X date."

THE PLANNING HORIZON

Before we begin developing your career HDD, we must play a chicken-and-egg game. There are two things we have to do at the same time: 1) set your planning horizon, and 2) define your HDD. Your planning horizon is the targeted end date of your HDD. It's the day your career objectives become reality. We use the word *horizon* because it implies some limitation on how far ahead it's possible to see.

It may be hard to wrap your head around the complexities involved with shaping your future if you don't have some hard and fast date to start with, but until you put forth the effort to describe that future as an HDD, it can be tough to pick a specific date toward which to plan. It's a chicken-and-egg problem. Which do you determine first, your planning horizon or your HDD?

We suggest that you choose your planning horizon first, then develop your HDD. Once you have developed your HDD, you can look back at the planning horizon you chose and ask, "Can I achieve my HDD by this date?" Perhaps you see that you can, or you may even determine that you can achieve your HDD in a shorter time frame. This is your career plan. Change it if you want to or need to. You are the only one responsible to it; and you are the only one accountable for its success or failure. You determine the time frame.

We can provide some general guidance on selecting a good planning horizon. If you are young, perhaps in your 20s, with a four-year term of service behind you, you may want to only plan out to three or five years. Because you are young, you may be starting out on a new profession that will require you to get additional schooling or accept an entry-level position in a particular industry. It is harder for you to see far into the future because you're less familiar with any particular career track. You also may not have decided what you want to do, and you'll likely learn more about your goals once you begin your professional life as a civilian. You may not know yourself well enough right now to plan the particulars of a career 10 years into the future, so keep your planning horizon short.

Perhaps you want to go into business for yourself; you want to be an entrepreneur. A good planning horizon for you would be the point at which you are ready to make that move to self-employment. That time is probably several years after your transition from active duty if you first need to develop experience in a particular industry or generate some capital to make your entrepreneurial move.

If you're transitioning out of the military after a longer career, setting a planning horizon 10 or 20 years out may be a good idea for several reasons, including more complex financial considerations, or family dependents. What are the big life events on your horizon? Do you have kids that will enroll in college in 5 or 10 years? That could be a good point to plan toward, considering the related financial demands. Perhaps you want to plan for retirement at a certain age, which means that your career HDD is the opposite of most people—it's when you want to end your career. We once asked a retired veteran about when he thought his planning horizon should be, and he responded, "Eternity." The point he was making was that his professional career was done, his children grown, and his future career focused on his legacy, accomplishing those goals that he believed were important to his community, his faith, and those around him. It was a new perspective for us, but we couldn't argue with his point. You can develop a legacy HDD as well as a career HDD. What's important to you?

Whatever your planning horizon may be, it should be determined on your own terms and according to your unique circumstances. Have a reason for picking a specific date. But remember that the future is unpredictable. None of us can tell with any certainty what's going to happen tomorrow. There are big-picture trends that we can predict with reasonable certainty, but not absolute confidence. However, setting your planning horizon out 40 years strains any reasonable boundaries. Remember, a successful military career with retirement benefits is 20 years. Little reason exists to plan beyond 20 years; if you do plan beyond that point, make sure you have some compelling reasons to do so. So, have you decided what your planning horizon is? Write it down on the career planning worksheet in Appendix B, or go to www.afterburnerdownrangeguide.com and start your career plan with your planning horizon. Write a specific day and year rather than just a year. Remember to list specifics rather than vague approximations. Specificity drives action. But write it in pencil! You may have to adjust that date.

THE CAREER KEY AREAS

What does your future career look like? Can you describe it in detail? There are many ways you might describe your professional life at your planning horizon, and peripheral aspects of your life can either complement your career or create conflicts. To create your future state with necessary detail, you should describe your career path in seven different key areas, which we will discuss in this chapter. We have listened to many veterans, and taken a poll of those we have hosted in our transition seminars. We have found that, typically, veterans describe only about two or three key areas when describing their future careers, so we have compiled a list of seven things to consider when developing your career plan. After we help veterans describe their career HDD in terms of each of these seven key areas, they found themselves much better equipped to plan well.

As a veteran, you are special. You bring unique assets to any employer; you've had experiences 99 percent of America will never have, so it's fine if you want to chuckle a bit as we introduce an acronym to help you remember the seven key areas. Here it comes: IAMSPeCiaL. Yes, that's right, you are special. We added the lower case *e*, *i*, and *a* to help all you hard-core warriors feel extra uncomfortable, but we are very serious about how important these seven key areas are. In short, the seven capital letters represent the following:

1. Interest/Industry
2. Advancement
3. Money/Compensation/Benefits
4. Security
5. People/Philosophy
6. Challenge
7. Location

Throughout the rest of this chapter, we will look more closely at these key areas, and educate you on some aspects of each that you may not know. Our intent is to help you be able to describe each of these seven key areas as it pertains to your unique desires and needs. When finished, you will have a high-definition description of the future career that you want. The detail that you put into it now will direct the strategic and tactical decisions and activities you must take to achieve it.

Example: Career High-Definition Destination (HDD)

Planning Horizon: December 31, 2022

Career HDD:

Interests/Industry: Employed by XYZ Corp. as learning and organizational development, leadership, coaching, and continuous improvement expert or executive with continuing opportunities for client interaction and the publication of written works (authorship).

Advancement: Scope of impact and responsibility remains stable or increases respective to the overall growth or XYZ Corp.; but opportunities exist for executive positions in the Learning and Development field outside of XYZ Corp.

Money/Compensation/Benefits: $150K avg. per annum in total compensation with 4% company-matched 401(k) contributions; high flexibility in working hours and locations; multiple opportunities to continue personal and professional development that is mutually beneficial to employer and self.

Security: Multiple options exist – remain with a growing and prosperous XYZ Corp.; or obtain position in L&D with a mature and stable firm; or undertake an entrepreneurial venture in private consultancy; or, assuming sufficient liquid capital, continue formal education in pursuit of a purely academic teaching career that leverages existing professional accomplishments.

People/Philosophy: Continue to enjoy the family-oriented culture of a small firm like that of XYZ Corp.

Challenge: Highly autonomous with considerable requirement for creative thinking and innovative productivity that is critical to the success of the organization.

Location: Reside in current or similar home in North GA with rural vacation residence in North GA or East NC mountains; option to work in home office; and travel no greater than 25%.

Figure 3.1   Example of a High-Definition Career Plan

Before we begin, take a look at what a complete HDD might look like in Figure 3.1. It's simply an example that demonstrates the level of detail and completeness you should aim to have.

The seven key areas, as we have arranged them, do not follow any particular order except for the first and the last. First is the *I* for your interests, or the industry that most interests you. We place this first because we've learned that if you are not involved in a career that interests you, you will not be engaged and energized enough to find success. The luckiest people often seem to be those who do what they enjoy—and make a living at it. We placed *L*, location, last because it shouldn't influence your HDD inordinately; we want you to formulate your HDD without location interfering. If where you choose to live after your transition from active duty is not in harmony with the other key areas of your HDD, you are handicapping your post-military career before it gets started.

We will address each of the seven key areas in turn. We ask that you consider each of them in isolation at first. Then, once you have drafted each of your seven related statements, consider them as a whole and refine them as needed.

Interests/Industry: What's Your Passion?

What engages your imagination? Do your interests drive you to a particular industry, or do they drive you to a particular profession? Also consider the skills you've learned in the military. Consider industries or jobs that combine your interests and skills, while realizing that perfect fits are hard to find. If you were in a military role you decidedly did not enjoy, this is the time to find something else.

While some military occupations can translate directly into civilian business, some do not. If you are an infantryman in the army or a boatswain's mate in the navy, your profession is strictly military-oriented. You have a greater challenge directly translating your skills into an interesting civilian career. You must determine what your interests are, and then either translate your abilities into what employers are seeking or develop new skills that are valued in the career that interests you.

One of the worst things that can happen to you on your career development journey is to accept a job and stick with it in spite of hating it. Too many vets take the first decently paying job that is offered to them, even though it may be something in which they have little interest or real aptitude. Then, after a short while, they decide to leave. Perhaps one day they just decide they've had enough and walk out the door without any warning to their employer. That is among the worst possible things that you can ever do in a civilian career; never leave an employer without at least two weeks of advance notice. Never leave an employer on bad terms. If there is anything that you can do to terminate your employment on positive terms, do it. Stick with a job until you have a plan and an opportunity to exit with class. There is a lot of truth to the old adage that it's easier to get a job when you already have one than to get a job when you are unemployed. If you leave an employer under anything less than positive terms, you will not have a good reference that you can provide to potential employers, and you will have employment experience on your resume that you won't want to discuss in an interview. If you think you are being clever by leaving a bad employment experience off your resume, potential employers will want to know what you did during that period. Gaps in employment history stick out like a sore thumb, so beware of a resume that shows you moving from one job to the next without any demonstration of career progression. Your objective when you transition from the service is to decide what kind of job you want so that you will begin developing a positive career path from the start.

Make the right choice from the beginning. Incorporate your interests and passions into your HDD. That vision will help you stay focused on a specific career path, and help prevent you from making a bad employment choice that will be difficult to recover from if it doesn't work out.

We have provided a blank worksheet in Appendix B and in your online worksheet. Below are several questions to stimulate your thinking process and a few simple examples of what key-area statements of interest might look like. You do not have to write a full paragraph or an eloquently worded statement of your passions. Just be sure to record the fundamentals important to you.

INTEREST QUESTIONS TO ANSWER:
1. What are my interests?
2. In what industries would I like to work?
3. In what industries do I have relevant skills that I enjoyed performing?

EXAMPLE KEY-AREA STATEMENTS:
- I am an executive in supply, logistics, and contracting in the small arms industry.
- I am free of a desk, working in the field as a supervisor in heavy industry or transportation.
- I write, publish, or market media services in the defense or recreational industries.

Your key-area statements should be composed in the present tense, such as "I am ..." rather than "I will be ...." In other words, your statement should be true at the planning horizon you selected rather than now. The point is to make your HDD a goal or objective to which you strive.

The key to composing key-area statements is to strike a balance between being narrow enough to drive action to your desired career goal, but broad enough to allow you the freedom to determine how you actually achieve it. On the one hand, if you state that you want to be the CEO of USAA, then you are limiting yourself because the actual achievability of such a goal depends on many uncontrollable forces. On the other hand, if you said that you want to be a senior executive in an international financial services company, you have an achievable goal without as many uncontrollable threats to its accomplishment. Realize that if you value your particular profession or job *function*, then you don't need to make any statement about preferred industry.

Advancement: Your Capacity for Future Growth

When you reach your planning horizon, have you achieved all your career goals? Probably not. By advancement we mean the capacity for further growth and development at your planning horizon. Growth and development up to that time is part of your career course of action, something we will address in Chapter 7. What you want to state in the advancement key area is that, at your planning horizon, you have further opportunities to develop your career. What new pathways will be available to you at that date?

There are many different ways to view advancement. There's growth and development potential. Are you positioned for further development or a new career transition? Perhaps you will be ready to make the move into self-employment. If so, what does that step look like?

Another important avenue for career development is through seeking lateral opportunities. Lateral changes in position can be an important component of career development where you won't necessarily move up the ladder, but you will gain important experience in some other area that allows you to ultimately advance in a monetary or hierarchical sense. Perhaps you want some industry experience and training so you can open your own business in the same or similar industry. If it's important to you, you may want to have access to a variety of mentors or coaches that will help you develop a career that would not necessarily be open to you until some other career milestone is met. You may even want to be a coach or mentor to others in your profession or industry.

Then, of course, there are the traditional aspects of advancement, which are marked by greater hierarchical positions and advances in pay. It's important to recognize that these are two different things, and that you may need to make specific statements to address each.

In your military experience, you were used to having structured guidance regarding what positions and experiences you needed in order to move to the next career position and remain competitive. As an army lieutenant, you may have started out as a platoon leader, then you moved to an executive officer (XO) position. If you were at the top of your game, you would get a chance to serve as a leader with a specialty platoon. As a captain, you knew you had to have a company command and then hoped to get a shot at being the S-3. Next, you could move into an XO role as a major before being selected for a battalion command as a lieutenant colonel. The civilian world is not so defined. Companies have different career paths for different positions, and the personnel organization can change at any time. Some companies may set clear progression requirements and schedules, whereas others allow career development to occur haphazardly. In most cases, you will need to set and develop your own path based on your company's opportunities.

Here are some questions you may want to ask yourself, followed by a few basic advancement key-area examples:

ADVANCEMENT QUESTIONS TO ANSWER:
1. What is my potential for advancement in pay and position?
   a. Do opportunities exist for me to advance within the organization?
   b. Are there clearly delineated pay scale increases?

2. What is my potential for continuing growth and development?
   a. Am I positioned for further development, career transition, or even retirement?
   b. Are there lateral development opportunities?
   c. Will development prepare me for becoming an entrepreneur?
   d. Are there coaching and mentoring opportunities or opportunities for me to become a coach or mentor to others?

EXAMPLE KEY-AREA STATEMENTS:
- I am an accomplished senior manager with significant opportunities to advance to executive management in a large corporation.
- I possess knowledge and experience to establish an entrepreneurial venture with the guidance of mentorship.

Money and Total Compensation: What Are Your Options?

In your military career you received a salary, a highly valuable benefits package that included inexpensive health and life insurance, generous paid time off, significant education benefits, a variety of special pay categories, and a retirement package that is tough to match in the civilian world. However, that total package of pay and benefits was static and uniform based upon your grade and time in service. In civilian employment, you will encounter an extremely varied array of compensation models.

Money may be one of the most significant components of your HDD, but we don't want you to think of just your paycheck; rather, consider total compensation. You might receive a paycheck that is the same every month or be compensated entirely by sales-based commissions. If you are interested in a part-time career, or if you are self-employed, you'll most likely be compensated on an hourly or contract basis. Bottom line: You may be compensated in a wide variety of ways, driven by many formulas.

Many benefits have significant impacts on total compensation. One of the largest will be health benefits; if you haven't already looked at your needs in this area, and just how expensive it can be, do that as soon as possible. The military provides great health benefits that few companies will match. In the military, you received four weeks of personal time off (PTO) and vacation each year. Most companies start at two or three weeks of total PTO. So, if you expect more, make sure that's part of your HDD, and, when you negotiate a position with an employer, make sure you include PTO in your compensation discussion. Compensation can also take the forms of year-end bonuses that are dependent upon a combination of your individual performance and the overall performance of the organization. In some executive positions, you may receive stock options and other revenue-sharing benefits, but those are becoming increasingly rare at the middle-management and associate-level positions. Also consider retirement benefits, which usually come in the form of matching 401(k) contributions from the employer. Fewer companies provide pension plans than in the past, and many of those that do are phasing them out. Also consider training and education as part of total compensation. Some companies will fund an advanced degree, which can be a huge benefit if such education fits in with your HDD.

Forms of intangible compensation might include how much exposure you get to others in your company and your overall industry. The kinds of people you will come in contact with can help you develop your career network—something we will address in detail in Chapter 5. Sometimes, the prestige of being associated with an employer's brand can present a huge opportunity, as others in your professional life may perceive working for a company like Apple or Nike as a real bonus. This can be especially important if it would be a benefit in the next steps of your HDD. For instance, could you leverage this experience in a new area or entrepreneurial pursuit?

Returning to the principal means of compensation, pay, many larger companies will set your initial salary within a pay band, a salary range within which persons in a job description must fall. It sets a minimum and maximum salary for any particular job. Unlike military pay charts, it would be rare for a company to disclose the exact dollar amounts of any particular pay band. It is also taboo, and usually prohibited by company policy, to disclose your or anyone else's pay rate, so do not discuss your pay with anyone but your immediate supervisor or an authorized representative of the employer's human resources department. Compensation in the civilian world is a private issue that is not openly discussed.

Salary is only one aspect of total compensation, though. For those in sales, the largest component of their total compensation is paid in the form of commissions on what they sell. The salary is, in many cases, a minor component of total compensation, while the bulk of pay comes as commissions. Today, the word *sales* is going out of style. Instead, sales professionals have moved toward calling themselves *business development professionals*. You may even see it abbreviated as BD. Although employees involved in business development may receive small salaries or no salaries at all, the monetary rewards can be very high for the successful BD professional.

Commission rates vary widely, depending on what is being sold. Sales associates at retail stores typically only make a few percentage points on what they sell, and many are only making just above an hourly minimum wage. In other high-end service industry sales, commissions can be around or greater than 10 percent. So, consider the math: If you get a 10 percent commission on what you sell, and the product you sell is in the range of $10,000 to $100,000, then you don't need to close a deal every day to make a very healthy living. It is possible that good business development professionals can make even more than the executives who run the company!

Corporate executives, however, generally get a much larger salary. They may also get very nice benefits packages that include things like:

- Executive health care plans that cover everything and charge no premium.
- Stock options that can mean huge monetary rewards in future years.
- Bonuses that can be a significant percentage of salary (or even more), and are paid based upon the company's overall performance or the executive's division's performance, as compared to a balanced scorecard.

Some entry-level and middle-management positions can receive benefits packages that are similar to executive packages, but this is becoming less and less common.

The point we want to make for you is that your base salary should not be everything you consider when you are negotiating to accept a new position with an employer. We have seen an O-3 accept a salary as an entry-level manager at a large company that was in the lower half of the pay band for him, and significantly less than his salary as a commissioned officer. Although this might not seem appealing, his performance incentives paid out up to 23 percent of his base salary, in addition to generous stock options that amounted to thousands of dollars in capital gains each year they matured. He received a retirement contribution on top of that. In the end, the total compensation in his civilian job exceeded his previous military compensation package.

Finally, there are positions that aren't executive, management, or sales. We call these technical positions. The compensation for technical positions is more like what you have been used to in the military. They may require specific, hard-to-acquire skill sets, and demand high pay rates. You basically just get paid to come to work and perform a function. If you do a good job, you'll get promoted into another pay band or get advanced to a higher rate within your pay band. In other words, you get a raise. These positions tend to have less total compensation than the others. The benefit to you is a steady income without a lot of variation. If that appeals to you, a technically oriented compensation model is what you want to have.

Figure 3.2 compares how many of the different compensation models may appear in total money and benefits. Realize that, depending on

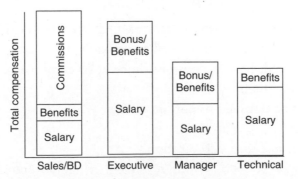

Figure 3.2   Sample Compensation Models

the company, position, industry, and profession, your total compensation will vary. You need to be aware of these different compensation models, determine what is right for you, and include the important aspects of that compensation model into your HDD.

Just like the military, some companies may offer a sign-on bonus. This may be an option that you can negotiate if the employer sees value in you but cannot justify giving you a larger salary. High salaries within a pay band can increase the organization's salary cap. A sign-on bonus gives the employee a good kick-start while also helping the company manage its payroll within a defined budget.

We are compelled to provide one final note about money for you to consider. Beyond subsistence and providing for the needs of your family and retirement, money is a poor gauge of success. If you believe that money is your principal motivator or that you plan to make as much money as possible as quickly as possible, so that you can take it easy for the remainder of your life, we urge you to be sure that you really know yourself. Most people who decide to chase the buck for all they are worth ultimately learn that it isn't worth it. Money is just one aspect of happiness.

In our live seminars that we provide to transitioning veterans, we have asked participants to rate what they consider to be the most important of the seven key areas in their HDDs. Not surprisingly, about one in three respondents say that interests/industry is the most important. Location follows as second, with about one in five indicating that where they want to live is the most important part of their future career. In contrast, less than one in 20 respondents say that money is their top concern!

MONEY/COMPENSATION/BENEFITS QUESTIONS TO ANSWER:

1. How much do I want/need to be paid?
   a. Salaried, hourly, commission only, or combination?
   b. How much?
2. What benefits are important to me?
   a. Health
   b. Personal time off/vacation
   c. Bonuses, stock options, revenue sharing, retirement, and so on

3. What training and education opportunities and benefits will I have?
4. What professional and public exposure or networking opportunities are desired?
5. Is positional or membership prestige important to me?
6. What perquisites are important, such as a company car or jet; office suite; and so on?

EXAMPLE KEY-AREA STATEMENTS:
- I earn a $250,000 salary with a 15 percent performance bonus, matching 401(k) contributions up to 5 percent, and stock options.
- I earn enough salary to meet my financial commitments while having a flexible work schedule to pursue my hobbies.
- I earn $90,000 minimum salary; company-funded executive MBA program at a top-25 business school or executive training at prestigious corporate facility (e.g., General Electric's Crotonville).

Security: Career Stability and How to Assess Risky Opportunities

Now let's consider security, the stability of your career. Is there a high or a low possibility that you will lose your job or that the profession you are in will become obsolete?

We like to use the term *risk appetite* for the level of insecurity or uncertainty you are willing to accept in a job. It also expresses the amount of effort required to jump the gap between your military and civilian careers. Are you willing to risk that level of change, the expenses of training and education, and the possibility that you may need to be unemployed or underemployed for some time? Are you interested in becoming an entrepreneur? Are you planning on making a full 180-degree turn into an entirely new career in which you have no experience? You may just want to continue doing the same sorts of things as a civilian that you did in the service—and that's a fine option; you can comfortably transition into something with which you're already familiar. You may be looking for a significant change, but first you want to get your feet on the ground.

Your risk appetite should also incorporate the stability of the industry, profession, or the particular company where you want to work. Are you in an industry with no obvious threatening trends? Or do you want to be on the edge of change in a start-up company where, on the one hand, you could realize long-term profits, or, on the other hand, see the company fold. Consider that, while the people who worked with Steve Jobs and Bill Gates as they started Apple and Microsoft retired millionaires, there are many, many more stories of start-ups that collapsed. You want to be most cautious about joining a company that is in a terribly troubled market and losing market share. Remember electronics retailer Circuit City, a once-stable icon? It went bankrupt in 2009. In fact, the entire retail electronics industry is going through significant changes. Are you willing to enter this industry right now? What's your risk appetite?

As you consider potential industries or professions in which you would like to work, do some research on how those industries and professions are trending. There is a website, indeed.com, that provides up-to-date information about job trends in any area of interest or geography.

Another important consideration is your skill variation; we call this *hedging*. If a chosen industry or profession turned out to be a bad choice, what ability do you have to rapidly transition to a different profession or industry? How employable are you across a wide variety of options? What careers could you pursue with your set of skills? Knowing those options makes for employment security, the ability to adapt to changing circumstances and survive.

Finally, you need to consider security versus money. Sometimes (not always), the more secure your position, the less money you'll make.

To be candid, you have probably been in a secure job for many years. Depending on what type of job or industry you choose for a civilian career, security boils down to whether or not you are making a contribution to the profitability of the company. If not, then your job could be in jeopardy. Human resources and training jobs tend to get cut first when a company's profitability begins to slip. The harder it is for a company to relate what you do directly to profits, the more likely it is for you to be cut or laid off when times get tough.

Senior executive positions can have a similar volatility. When you are near the top, you have a greater impact on a company's success. So, if success doesn't happen, there's always someone who will hold you accountable. This is the modern business world and it's not like the latter half of the 20th century when loyalty kept individuals securely employed for decades. Most companies have a "what have you done for me lately" mentality; if you don't adjust to this new reality, you may have a difficult time. We have seen vice presidents who have been with an organization for 18 years, only to be out the door when a new CEO comes in and changes the management team. It's just the nature of the business, and you need to be aware of the corporate culture. We don't mean to scare you—just inform you.

We have mentioned start-ups and mature businesses, which are two parts of the same life cycle. It is important to understand this life cycle for several reasons. First, you need to understand how volatile your new environment may be. Second, you should recognize how the skills and abilities that you gained in the military can be of value to a company in any particular phase of its life cycle. The life cycle of a typical company is illustrated in Figure 3.3, although the time scale can be a few years to even a century or more. Most businesses ultimately

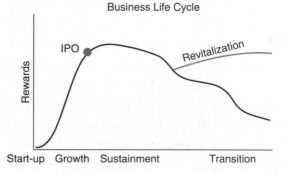

Figure 3.3 Possible Business Life Cycle

transition or die; very few companies have been around for more than a century.

Every business begins as a start-up. And oftentimes, businesses that have been around for many years may revitalize and go through a new start-up phase. For example, companies can spin off business units that become new entities but retain the backing of the parent company's infrastructure, brand, and national presence. Their culture is that of a start-up, but they are far more stable, and incorporate the revolutionary technological changes that the 21st century has brought to their industry. Start-ups can have both huge upsides and downsides; regardless, the amount of work that is generally required to get start-ups going and growing can be very high. The work-life balance may be skewed toward work. You need to have a passion for the business to remain focused and successful in a start-up.

The talents that you might bring to a start-up can be very valuable if you are able to demonstrate them to an employer. If you have led troops in battle, you certainly can lead through ambiguity. Start-ups require a lot of leadership in a highly ambiguous and chaotic environment. The learning curve is high in start-ups because a small number of employees must figure out how best to run the business and how to carve out a profitable niche in their market. Your skills at organizing and planning may be essential to a start-up, whereas the precision of your military-style communication will be critical. You can help the team understand who is doing what, why, and when so team members are not wasting time. Finally, in such a chaotic and highly demanding environment, discipline is essential, just like the military regimen that you developed during your time in the service. You have a military work ethic. You are used to working around the clock. If that is something you are content with, then a start-up might be a good fit for you.

Notice that in our outline of the skills needed in a start-up, we mentioned skills like leadership, organization, communication, and discipline (see Figure 3.4). We hope that you recall the LOCKED on Teams model that we introduced in Chapter 2. As we move forward, we will be referencing this model more and more. As we review the life cycle stages of a business, we will highlight those LOCKED skill sets that are most relevant to a business at that particular stage.

Start-up Phase	Growth Phase	Sustainment Phase/ Maturity	Transition Phase—Exit/ Merger
Leadership	Leadership	Leadership	Leadership
Organization	Organization	Organization	Organization
Communication	Communication	Communication	Communication
Knowledge	Knowledge	Knowledge	Knowledge
Experience	Experience	Experience	Experience
Discipline	Discipline	Discipline	Discipline

Figure 3.4 LOCKED Skill Sets for the Major Stages of Business Development

If a business survives its start-up stage, it moves into a growth stage. You may find great opportunities for your talents in a company that is in a period of growth. Companies in a growth phase need leadership to execute their plans. Further, growth means hiring new people, training them, and developing them into high-performing teams, just like you have done in the military. You come from an environment where the turnover rate is extremely high due to standard tour rotations. Approximately every three years, the personnel in any given unit turn over completely. That's much higher than anything that you will generally find in the civilian sector. Just like in the start-up phase of a business, growth also requires the organization and discipline to train and manage that turnover.

If growth is successful, a business can enter a sustainment stage, which takes shape as the 8-to-5, Monday-through-Friday workweek. Companies in a sustainment phase are mature and tend to have a greater degree of security, but what you will often find in these companies is the need to decrease waste and inefficiency. Knowledge and experience are important for mature businesses to help them maintain efficiency while innovating and getting new products to market quickly. You may have had some experience in process improvement in your military career. So, be careful to consider how you might phrase and detail such experiences in terms of process and continuous improvement in your resume. A company that is mature and in sustainment is probably going to have bureaucratic institutions and standards similar to the military. Veterans, by virtue of experience in such an environment, are masters of handling bureaucracy, and we don't use the word *bureaucracy* in a negative way. Bureaucracies can be essential to managing and running corporations.

Finally, there are companies that are in transition, nearing the end of their life cycles—at least in their present form. They may be in a dying or radically changed market and have failed to adapt effectively; they may be targets for acquisition or bankruptcy. You would do well to avoid companies like this unless you want the demanding challenge of helping such a company make a turn-around or transition to a new stage.

There are also healthy companies that are transitioning into a new form. They may be merging, or the owners or board of directors may be interested in selling the company and finding leadership to get the business in top shape for the sale. Regardless, change leadership is an essential skill for companies in transition. You may have some significant experience in leading and managing change; of course, integrity, accountability, and organizational skills are also important during transitions.

With that summary of the life cycle of a business, do you know where the company you are interviewing with is on the graph depicted in Figure 3.3? No one may know for certain, but what do you suspect from available news and information? Considering the context of each phase, is it the place for you?

Finally, notice the dot labeled *IPO* on the graph. An IPO is an initial public offering, in which a privately held company opens itself up to investment by becoming publicly traded, which means that investors can buy stock in the organization. IPOs often occur during a growth phase. An IPO is a major transformation for any company. It means that public investors are now the owners rather than its creators or founders. Much change can occur before and after an IPO. Think about your skills as a veteran, when you had to succeed a leader or create new policies or procedures in your unit. These types of shifts are common in an IPO transition of a business.

Now that you have an understanding of the basic life cycle of a business, you also need to understand the basic legal forms of a business. Understanding how an employer is legally classified will help steer your career decisions and make security-related judgments. What do we mean by legal classification? What's the legal difference between Wal-Mart, a local independent sporting goods store, and a small law firm?

The independent sporting goods store is most likely a sole proprietorship, meaning it has a single owner who is liable for the business, including the store and everything in it. Your risk appetite should be high if you are entertaining thoughts of working for a sole proprietorship. Employment opportunities for such businesses should be fully aligned with your HDD.

Many organizations choose to incorporate as limited liability companies, or LLCs. LLCs are new legal entities that did not exist in most states until the late 1990s, so we are seeing more and more of these, particularly smaller companies (though they can be large global companies as well). LLCs have fewer regulatory compliance requirements associated with them in comparison to corporations.

Wal-Mart, on the other hand, is in fact a corporation. Corporations are what most of you consider big businesses to be, although a small company can be a corporation as well. A corporation is a legal entity unto itself, and its owners and employees are not personally liable for its debts. It can also have investors to provide growth capital—something a proprietorship cannot do. Corporations, especially large ones, are almost always overseen by a board of directors. In most cases, the board hires a CEO to run the business and select a management team, and in some cases the CEO may also have a key position on the board. These are the types of businesses that we think typically provide the greatest security and stability, since they are heavily regulated by our government, and not closely tied to the fate of a few individual owners. However, smaller corporations, which may be classified as S corporations, can, along with LLCs, provide great opportunities. S corporations have fewer legal requirements than other corporations, which makes them easier to manage, but they also have considerable IRS oversight. If you want to work in a small company, an S corporation is a usually a safe choice.

SECURITY QUESTIONS TO ANSWER:
1. What's my risk appetite?
   a. Am I making a professional transition into a field where I have little or no training or experience? What will that cost in time and money?
   b. Am I doing the same sort of job—just turning in my uniform for civvies?
2. What's the stability of the profession or industry that I desire to enter over the period of my planning horizon?
   a. Is it a mature industry with few or no foreseeable threatening trends?
   b. Is it an emerging industry or profession with an uncertain future?
   c. Is it a profession or industry that is declining, dying, or suffering turbulent change?
3. Do I have a versatile set of skills that provide employment opportunities in a variety of industries or professions?
4. How important is my pay versus my long-term security?

EXAMPLE KEY-AREA STATEMENTS:
- I have remade my professional self at substantial cost, but with long-term job and income stability.
- I have made a seamless transition from a military to a civilian career, and established a position in a stable profession and company.
- I have established a new set of skills and experiences that leverage multiple career options.

People and Philosophy: Finding Fit

As you transition out of the military, you are leaving an extraordinary cadre of people with a shared philosophy of service to country. For many of you, leaving military service is a tough choice because, above all else, serving with your brothers and sisters in arms has been a cherished and rewarding experience. For others, you may be eager to move away from the military lifestyle and environment. As you begin your civilian career, who are the people you want to work with? What is the mission, purpose, or philosophy of your future employer? What is the cultural experience that you seek in your HDD?

Within your HDD, people or philosophy helps you determine what sort of career community you want to be a part of. Philosophy, the inward purpose of an organization, has become a big subject in businesses today because it's so closely connected to brand and the outward purpose of an organization. Companies such as Starbucks, Apple, Nike, and Harley-Davidson have corporate philosophies and cultures that directly relate to the brands, products, or services they provide. Those are the companies that have recognizable cultures, which makes it much easier for us to judge whether we fit with them. Other companies may have internal cultures and philosophies that are more difficult to discern. It's important to meet with as many people within a company as possible during the interview process, so that you can gauge these important aspects of an organization.

For example, we worked with a former U.S. Army Ranger who served with the 101st Airborne and chose to become an investment banker on Wall Street. He achieved that career goal, but a year later he was ready to quit. He had joined an organization that did not provide him the same culture or satisfaction he found in the military. This soldier did not have specific situational awareness of the firm he joined. The result was a misalignment between his expectations and the realities of his career choice.

Perhaps there is an even more important question that you have to ask yourself: Do you want to work with other people? If so, what kind of people? Are you willing to go beyond your comfort zone and work with people who you must collaborate with and trust, despite their being very different from you? People who you have served with in the military may have very different backgrounds, but despite that, you have a lot in common with each other. All of you chose to serve in the military, a very rare choice for a very select kind of person. That makes servicemen and women much more alike than you might first consider. In business settings, you may be challenged by people with entirely different values and ways of perceiving the world. You have to adapt and treat people like esteemed colleagues.

Consider your personality and temperament and how these aspects of your personality impinge upon your success in the business world. By virtue of our choice to pursue military service in the first place, veterans will often fall into the left two quadrants of the graph in Figure 3.5. You have probably had a personality or temperament survey performed in the past, and have some idea of where you fall within the four basic categories (although some tests have eight types and some go as far as sixteen or more). Some of the more popular typing systems use titles like you see in each of the quadrants in Figure 3.5. The adjectives you see in each quadrant will help you identify which type you are.

Few of us fall entirely within a single quadrant, and some people have strong tendencies in all four quadrants. Since you're about to choose a new career, you should know yourself well so you can choose a job in which you're predisposed to succeed.

In general, you should choose industries and professions that are aligned with your type. In Figure 3.6, we indicated in bold some of the types of industries and professions that align well with each of the four key personality types. We have also put the professions and industries that those personality types may find challenging in italics. If you have a strong tendency toward any single quadrant, you would be wise to avoid the professions or positions italicized in that quadrant.

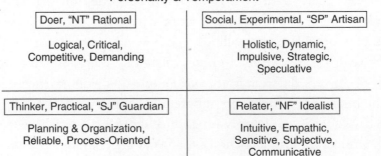

Figure 3.5 Common Professional Personality Types

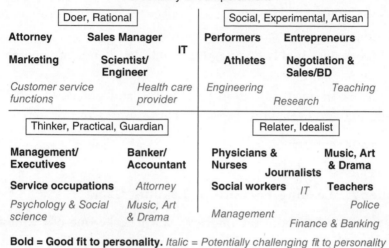

Bold = Good fit to personality. *Italic = Potentially challenging fit to personality*

Figure 3.6 Professional Matches by Personality Type

Networking can be another challenge for veterans transitioning into the business world. Veterans often have less well-defined personal networks, but networking is a critical skill for developing one's career and obtaining great positions. Although networking can be a severe weakness for vets, remember that the military tends to attract people who are in the left two quadrants of the personality spectrum whereas networking is a talent set that tends toward the right side of the spectrum. So, some veterans may have underdeveloped career networks when compared to their civilian counterparts.

MONEY/COMPENSATION/BENEFITS QUESTIONS TO ANSWER:

1. Is the philosophical purpose behind the industry or profession you are seeking important and, if so, what is it?
2. What sort of people do you want to work with?
   a. Do you like working with people?
   b. Do you want to work in a highly diverse team or with highly diverse customers/clients?
   c. Do you want to work with people like you?
3. How does your personality fit into your chosen industry or profession?

EXAMPLE KEY-AREA STATEMENTS:
- I work with people with a similar background who esteem integrity, service, and duty to others.
- I work with highly diverse people who challenge my beliefs and values.
- I work in an organization with values and objectives I believe in and am engaged to support. Those values and objectives are _____.

Challenge: Leaning Forward or Leaning Back

What drove you to join the military? Was it to be one of the best of the best? To be part of an elite team? Was it to face and overcome challenges that only military service offers? Did those challenges provide personal growth and engaging purpose? Do you wish to continue having your limits pressed? Or, have you had enough challenge in your professional career? Perhaps you have interests or obligations in your life that are not directly related to your professional career, but require a great deal of challenge, which means your career needs to be, in simple terms, "easy."

But, easy or hard is not the best way to look at the meaning of challenge. To describe the level of challenge that you want to have in your career HDD, think in terms of two criteria: responsibility and autonomy. You have probably had some significant level of responsibility in your military career, particularly in the higher levels of leadership. That responsibility may have been for lives, materiel, or even money. Others counted on you to perform your job and be accountable for some degree of reliable performance. Autonomy, on the other hand, may not have been something that you thought you experienced in your military career. Autonomy is an expression of the level of freedom that you have to carry out your duties. If your boss says, "I don't care how you do it, just get it done," he is granting you autonomy. If you are self-employed, you have a large degree of autonomy to choose what you do and when you do it—but you must respond to your clients, customers, employees, and the bottom line.

Typically, if one has a high degree of responsibility, then one should have an equivalent level of autonomy, but that is not *always* true. One can have enormous responsibilities, but have very little ability to choose how those responsibilities are met. For example, an engineer operating the nuclear reactor on an aircraft carrier may have enormous responsibility but a very restrictive set of standards to operate the reactor. In the business world, a similar situation might be that of a plant manager who has a responsibility to produce a product in a specified way. A plant manager has a high level of responsibility, but typically cannot decide how to reorganize, restructure, or retool the plant based on personal decisions. Other people often set the methods for a plant's operation, albeit with input from the manager. Others in the creative or innovative aspects of a business, such as research and development, may have challenges that can be described as having high autonomy but low responsibility. Research and development is often an experimental branch of a business, where outputs are hoped for but not necessarily delivered—a low level of responsibility to the bottom line.

So, how do you describe your level of responsibility and autonomy in your career HDD? Are you a check-out clerk at Wal-Mart with a low level of autonomy and responsibility? Or, are you an executive of a Fortune 500 company with responsibility for thousands of employees and millions in revenue, but the autonomy to lead that workforce and drive revenue according you your own autonomous decisions? Can you describe your career challenge as a mix of autonomy and responsibility? Perhaps you work as a freelance writer who accepts responsibility only for writing projects that you select and, thus, maintains high autonomy in your employment choices.

If autonomy and responsibility do not quite express the level of challenge that you want to set for yourself, consider one more dimension: impact. Impact is a level of challenge that drives a step beyond. Impact is really about your value. You can be a highly autonomous corporate manager and have low impact; or, you can have little autonomy, in a strict sense, and no responsibility, and become an organization's most valued member. In a way, impact is a valuation of your legacy. Someone who has impact can be at any level of autonomy and responsibility and yet have an enormous impact on an organization, or even society as a whole. Perhaps you want the challenge of becoming a leader who has great influence.

CHALLENGE QUESTIONS TO ANSWER:
1. Am I on cruise control or am I leaning forward?
2. How much autonomy do I seek?
    a. Is it a highly structured environment with low autonomy?
    b. Is it an unstructured or entrepreneurial environment with high autonomy?
3. What level of responsibility do I seek?
    a. Do I have little responsibility for anyone but myself and the tasks assigned to me?
    b. Am I an executive with a vast scope of powers, people, and responsibilities?
4. What is my impact on the organization—or even beyond it?
    a. Am I worth little more than my total compensation?
    b. Am I a top talent asset?
    c. Will my legacy live beyond me with reverence and awe?

EXAMPLE KEY-AREA STATEMENTS:
- I am the CEO of a disruptive industry upstart or a leader of the largest and most innovative business unit of a Fortune 500 company.
- I am a highly innovative and unique high-value contributor to a high-performing team.
- I am respected for my contributions (in other words, you do your job and go home to things that are more important to you than your career).

Location: Home, the Unspoken Threat to Your Career

As we suggested at the introduction to the HDD key areas, location is one of the most important. If you decided where you were going to live once you leave active duty without considering all the other key areas in your career HDD, then you may have made a poor decision.

If you are truly interested in developing a specific career with all the detail that you have put into the first six key areas of your HDD, then you must not allow this last key area to drive the rest. You need to understand what industries and opportunities are open to you as a function of geography.

Do you want to be an executive in the financial industry? Well, you should consider relocating to New York City, Charlotte, San Francisco, or any of several other major cities that function as banking centers.

Do you want a technical position in an automobile manufacturing plant? Well, you may want to consider living in a more rural setting in the Southeast because many major automobile plants are located in places like Spartanburg, South Carolina (BMW); West Point, Georgia (Kia); or Bowling Green, Kentucky (Chevrolet). More and more often, automobile manufacturers are opening operations in the rural or small-city south. Our point is that you should know what geographies align with your career HDD.

In our training of veterans, we have recognized an alarming trend. Many veterans decide where they are going to live before considering all of their career options. Spouses are often a factor driving this decision. After all, many military spouses have put up with multiple relocations throughout the course of a long military career, and too often, veterans fail to account for what might be best—for their spouse, family, and themselves—in their post-military career. For instance, if you made a promise to your spouse or family to return to a small town that is 100 miles from the nearest city, then you have to recognize how that affects your career options—and the life you share.

With that in mind, there are some aspects about location that you may not have considered. Can you work in your chosen career field from home? We live in an age where telecommuting work is becoming more common. If not, ask yourself if you can live in a rural setting and commute a few days each week to an office. Perhaps you can spend the workweek in a distant office or city, where you have a place to live Monday through Friday. If so, how far is your chosen place of residence from a major airport so you can easily get to work on

Monday morning and back home on Friday afternoon? Our point is that you must very carefully consider your options regarding your choices of location and how those choices affect your other career objectives.

There are other aspects of location that you should consider as well: What sort of physical accommodations or environment surround you in your career HDD? Do you work out of your pick-up truck, in a high-rise office building, or in a suburban office park?

How much travel are you willing to do and where? It's not as glamorous as some people think. Most people consider regular business travel to have a negative impact upon their quality of life. We know many people who have passed up significant career opportunities because they did not view the travel requirements as acceptable. Always ask about the travel requirements for a potential job, and know what your limits are.

How far do you have to commute to work every day and, if you are working in a metropolitan area, what is the impact of traffic? What's your proximity to other important services and locations to your home—your church, schools, and other family support and services? Have you considered your proximity to a VA hospital and whether or not that is important to you?

LOCATION QUESTIONS TO ANSWER:
1. In what geographic area do I wish to work and live? Are they different?
   a. CONUS/OCONUS/foreign or exotic location
   b. Region/state
   c. City/suburban/country/isolated (need an ATV or dogsled to get there)
2. What are the accommodations of my workspace?
   a. Office park/high rise/home office
   b. Work out of my car or in the field
3. Do I commute and, if so, how? What are the travel requirements for my job?
4. What's my proximity to non–career-related things like family, schools, church, and so on?

EXAMPLE KEY-AREA STATEMENTS:
- Reside in a secluded lakeside mountain cabin with home office in Colorado while conducting <50% business travel.
- Reside in suburban area zoned with top-rated school; within 25 miles of major airport and place of work.

We hope that you have drafted your own statements that address the seven key areas that we have outlined here. If not, stop and do that before you continue on to the next chapter. By detailing the future career that you aspire to, you have accomplished a significant step toward achieving it. If you are unsure about some of the statements you have drafted, that's fine. Think about your career HDD for a while. Ask family and friends what they think, and remember that you can always change your career HDD as you learn new things.

The career HDD that you have created will now help you plan further. You know what your future should look like, but you are not yet ready to describe the specific tasks or objectives to accomplish your HDD. You must first consider the threats to achieving it, the obstacles that stand in your way. In the next chapter, we will help you identify some of those threats.

CHAPTER DEBRIEF

- Determine your planning horizon, the date that you will plan your career high-definition destination (HDD).
- Develop a career HDD based upon seven key areas that, together, provide the high-definition nature of your career goals. The seven key areas follow the IAMSP*e*C*ia*L acronym for:
  - **Industry/Interests:** What interests you? What are you passionate about doing?
  - **Advancement:** At your planning horizon, what options for advancement do you have?

(continued)

(continued)

- **Money/Compensation/Benefits:** How and to what extent are you compensated?
- **Security:** How secure is your career? What is your appetite for risk?
- **People/Philosophy:** How do you describe the people and the environment in which you work?
- **Challenge:** What level of autonomy, responsibility, and/or impact do you wish to have?
- **Location:** How do you describe the physical location and environment in which you work?

CHAPTER 4

IDENTIFY THE THREATS

SIX STEPS OF PLANNING

1. Determine the mission objective.
2. **Identify the threats**.
3. Identify your resources.
4. Evaluate lessons learned.
5. Develop a course of action.
6. Plan for contingencies.

Abraham Lincoln was a man of extraordinary wisdom and political acumen. As leader of a nation embroiled in civil war, he successfully navigated a treacherous path through many tragic years of battle, division within his own cabinet, and powerful opposition in Congress. By his death, he had achieved the legal abolition of slavery and an end to the war, but the path to get there was anything but straight. With your career high-definition destination (HDD) clear in your mind, you have probably found yourself wondering exactly how you are going to get to it. What is the path?

We hope you have had an opportunity to view the film *Lincoln*,[1] which was released in 2012 and starred Daniel Day Lewis as the

---

[1] Steven Spielberg and Kathleen Kennedy (Producers) & Steven Spielberg (Director). (October 8, 2012) *Lincoln*. United States: Walt Disney Studios.

United States' 16th president. If you have, you may recall a remarkable dialogue between Lincoln and Thaddeus Stevens (portrayed by Tommy Lee Jones). Lincoln says:

> A compass, I learnt when I was surveying, it'll, it'll point you true north from where you're standing, but it's got no advice about the swamps and deserts and chasms that you'll encounter along the way. If in pursuit of your destination you plunge ahead, heedless of obstacles, and achieve nothing more than to sink in a swamp, what's the use of knowing true north?

In your military experience, did you ever plunge ahead heedless of the obstacles that stood in your way? Certainly not. In this chapter, we will introduce you to the second step to planning, identifying the threats or obstacles that stand in the way of achieving your HDD. If you served in combat arms in the U.S. Army, you may recognize this planning step as similar to the "Enemy Forces" component of a standard operations order (OPORD). What are the enemy's capabilities and how will that impact me? Step Two of our career-planning strategy asks what could impede you in achieving the career HDD that you have set as your objective.

With detail around the seven key areas of your HDD, we hope that it becomes much easier for you to identify the threats that stand in your way. For example, did the consideration of your location help you realize obstacles such as cost of living, transit, or proximity to career opportunities? Is there a gap between the average compensation of jobs aligned to your career interests and the total benefits you need or desire?

As you consider the threats and obstacles to your career success, consider them in two categories: controllable and uncontrollable. Controllable threats fall within your power or ability to influence. You can negate, mitigate, or avoid them. For example, if you seek a career position that requires an advanced degree that you do not possess, then you can negate that threat by obtaining that degree. You might also mitigate the requirement for an advanced degree by developing significant and compelling experience that could be considered degree-equivalent. Many job descriptions indicate experiences that are an acceptable substitute for formal education. You can also avoid such requirements by seeking career opportunities that do not demand such a degree. Remember Jim Skinner, the former CEO of McDonald's, who was an enlisted veteran? He headed a major corporation and, unlike most of his peers, he did not possess a college degree! Many threats fall within your personal ability to influence, but some threats can be very challenging to overcome. Obtaining a management position without an undergraduate degree in most major companies is becoming more and more difficult. Although you should be reasonable in determining what threats you can or cannot control, be creative and persistent in probing for ways to mitigate or avoid those threats.

Uncontrollable threats are truly beyond your control. Perhaps there were military career options that you were prevented from pursuing because of some physical disqualification. In your civilian career, you may encounter similar requirements that you simply cannot meet. If you desire to be the vice president of finance for a major company one year after you transition from active duty, but you do not have an undergraduate degree, experience in the industry, or a CPA license, there is simply no way that you can achieve such a position in so short a period of time. Along those lines, there are jobs that require certifications beyond formal education that are legally or professionally required before you can obtain such a position. You must be able to identify these threats before moving forward in your career planning.

There are also uncontrollable events that can inhibit progress toward your career HDD. What are they, and what will you do about them? What is your contingency plan if those events come to pass? Those threats can be personal, life-changing issues that involve the health and welfare of family members. Uncontrollable threats might also be the loss of a job for any number of reasons such as layoffs or even the dissolution or bankruptcy of a company. Almost everyone should recognize job loss as a threat to achieving their career HDD. We will address how to deal with those contingencies in the last step of planning in Chapter 7. For now, we simply want to identify the threats to our HDD and decide whether they are controllable or uncontrollable.

Example Threats					
	C	U		C	U
Yourself and your family's needs	X		Flatness and Lack of Uniforms	X	
Virtual Signature	X		Language and General Knowledge	X	
OPSEC and Recruiters	X		Civilian – Military Misperceptions		X
Resumes	X		Applicant Tracking systems (ATS)	X	
Interviewing Skills	X				

Figure 4.1 Example Threats

Are you not sure what the threats may be? Well, we cannot tell you all the threats that stand in the way of your personal and unique career HDD, but we can address some of the common threats, including many that you may not have considered.

In Figure 4.1 you will see some of those common threats. Notice that we have identified them as controllable or uncontrollable. We will discuss each in turn.

THREAT #1: YOU!

You can be the biggest threat to finding success with your HDD! Do you know what you want? Do you know what your spouse and family want? Sometimes that is even more significant a factor—or obstacle—in starting your civilian career. What about your temperament and personality? How aligned is your personality with your relationships and the career you've chosen?

The older and wiser we become, the better we know ourselves. A significant change in career presents many uncertainties. As you transition, you'll likely learn more about yourself, and that can help further develop your HDD.

We highly recommend you take a personality assessment like Myers–Briggs or the Kiersey Temperament Survey (KTS), found in *Please Understand Me II* by former fighter pilot David Keirsey. By understanding your personality better, you can ensure that you don't become your own biggest threat by pursuing an HDD and career that is misaligned with your core self. We recommend you read the entire book so that you gain an understanding of all the variety of personalities that you will encounter in your work and in your life. It is a great resource and a step forward in your personal development as a leader.

THREAT #2: YOUR VIRTUAL SIGNATURE

Just a decade ago, acts could be momentary, and statements fleeting. Today, however, we all have permanent records that exist on the Internet. We call that permanent record your *virtual signature*.

What happens if someone were to type your name into an Internet search engine and hit enter? If you have a good virtual signature, a potential employer will probably get a list that includes entries on sites such as LinkedIn or Facebook. Be aware of your social media privacy settings, and be sure to adjust them to prevent potential employers from seeing anything that could cast doubt on your professionalism or judgment. This is especially important when it comes to personal information, photos, and posts.

Although studies differ on the exact number, they agree that more than one third of employers research your virtual signature as part of the hiring and selection process. The results of their research should substantiate and reiterate the information on your resume and provide some other positive and amplifying information about you and how well you would fit in their company. If you have a great virtual signature, that employer might see that you have a professional blog that presents your skills and abilities in a very positive light. Perhaps there are news stories about your previous successes that reinforce everything on your resume. If that's the case, you have done well to cultivate a virtual signature that positively represents you. Many employers will check your virtual signature before they consider bringing you in for an interview, so ignore this threat at your peril.

If your virtual signature is anything but what a potential employer hopes to see, you have missed a huge opportunity to represent yourself and build your personal brand. Your brand should be represented in the virtual world and it should be genuine. Your virtual signature or brand should enable a potential employer to gauge how well you would fit in their organization.

We believe that the days of the resume are numbered. Resumes are designed to represent you as you want a potential employer to see you. Unfortunately, a one- or two-page resume cannot tell the whole story of you. That's what interviews are for. Your virtual signature can provide a potential employer with much more detail while, at the same time, validating your qualifications—something a resume cannot do.

You probably have a Facebook profile. But do you have a LinkedIn profile? If not, you must get to work on developing a LinkedIn profile now! LinkedIn is a rapidly developing and changing platform for professional social networking. It is already beginning to take over as a principal means for employers and recruiters to search for talent. No doubt, some of the applications and structure of LinkedIn will have changed by the time this book is published. We will discuss how to leverage the basics of LinkedIn in Appendix L because it is so important. The bottom line, though, is that if you are not using LinkedIn now and beginning to develop a professional virtual signature, you must get started. Your lack of a positive virtual signature is a significant threat to your career development. This book will help address that threat.

THREAT #3: OPSEC AND RECRUITERS

Although a lack of a positive virtual signature is a threat to you, having your personal information posted in virtual space can also be a threat. We recommend that you exercise good operational security (OPSEC) on social networking sites like Facebook and LinkedIn, and when posting your resume and other information on job sites.

If you are transitioning off active duty and seeking your first civilian job, there is no danger in posting that fact on job boards and on your social networking sites. You want everyone to know that you are seeking an opportunity, but if you already have a civilian job and have chosen to begin looking for another career opportunity, you should be very careful. Remember that we live in a time where most any information that you seek is available if you know what you are looking for. Add to that the high connectivity of networks of people and the speed of communication. In today's world, secrets are hard to keep. If you post your resume on a job site or blatantly indicate that you are in the job market (which you can easily do on LinkedIn), assume that everyone, including your current employer, will know that very quickly. In some cases that may be what you want, but in most cases it will compromise or even jeopardize your current job status and security.

We recommend that you only post on job sites that allow you to post a resume without your name or other personal information, except for a cell phone number and a private e-mail address. You will also want to omit the name of your current employer on your resume and keep identifying information out of the description of your current position. Of course, your work history can still give away your identity to those that know you well, but using some basic OPSEC will make that very difficult.

Keeping personally identifying information off your job postings will also help protect you from a few unscrupulous recruiters that can take advantage of you. How can they do this? Imagine that you post your resume on a job-seeking site with your name and the name of your current employer. Because recruiters usually work within an industry, they may notice when companies in their industry have employees that post for job opportunities. Although it would be unethical, a morally compromised recruiter could contact your current employer, let them know that you are looking for another job and offer their services to replace you. The recruiter could also reach out to you and offer their services to place you. If they already know of a position that you may be a good fit for, they can squat on that position by getting a signed agreement from that employer and cut you off from the opportunity if you do not work through them. The end result is that you are put in an awkward position with your current employer, a good opportunity for you may be eliminated, and the recruiter gets to collect placement fees from both employers. A recruiter could even attempt to get you to sign a placement contract and attempt to charge you directly for placement services. You should never agree to pay a recruiter. Good recruiters with high integrity will not charge the job seeker; they make money by charging companies.

Recruiters can be a great resource for you. There are many good ones and poor ones. Be careful in selecting a recruiter if you choose to seek their help. In Chapter 5 we will address how to identify a good recruiter.

THREAT #4: FLAT HIERARCHY AND FIT

We noted in Chapter 1 that there are significant hierarchical distinctions between military service and business and that you must begin to transition your mindset accordingly. The significant transition that you must make is to recognize that you will not have a prescribed uniform of the day that you will put on every morning. You are going to have to maintain your own wardrobe that adheres to either a company-published dress code or to an unspoken dress code that fits the culture of the business.

The lack of a uniform can create an uncomfortable atmosphere for a veteran when it is accompanied by a flat hierarchy and a difficulty to distinguish rank and position. You may not get a brief by a new employer that clearly establishes the reporting relationships between you and everyone else your work with. When one navy veteran first took on a management position in a business, he knew who his boss was, and he knew who reported to him. But, because he was the youngest person on the management team and he had not received any clear direction on the reporting relationships of the rest of the team, he took orders from most everyone on that team. One manager in particular dropped by on a near-daily basis to provide instruction and to issue orders. The veteran had the impression that the manager was the equivalent of an executive officer (XO) or second-most senior leadership position next to his boss, the general manager. Eventually, the GM called the vet into his office and said, "Forget about what that guy tells you to do; you report to me." Our point is that you need to ask questions about reporting relationships because just because someone holds a more senior position, it doesn't mean that everyone under them must follow their orders. These relationships are also not likely to be obvious by looking at what people are wearing.

Along these same lines, relax a bit. It's obvious when we encounter recently transitioned veterans in a business. They are the ones who say "Yes, ma'am" and "Yes, sir" to everyone. Their hair still conforms to military regulations. They might wear a few components of the uniform they used to wear on active duty such as black leather or patent leather shoes, or even a standard issue brass belt buckle. You are going to have to get used to dressing for a less structured and more flexible atmosphere. You need to quickly judge the culture and atmosphere of the business you join and adapt to the way they do things.

THREAT #5: LANGUAGE AND GENERAL KNOWLEDGE

The business world, like the military, is full of jargon and acronyms. Acronyms and terminology can even vary among service branches. Moreover, there is jargon and acronym-laden language inside the communities within each of the services. It is no different in businesses.

As we interact with businesses each day in our work, we are constantly reminded of the language and knowledge barrier that exists between us and our clients. That is not a significant issue for us because our clients do not expect us to understand their business and industries at the same level that they do, but they do expect us to have a high level of general knowledge and literacy. Such literacy is particularly important if you intend to secure a management position in a company.

The best way to develop your language and general knowledge is by gathering information on the specific industry or interests that you identified in your HDD. Chances are that there are websites, blogs, professional organizations, books, and magazines that address your particular areas of interest. Are you interested in a career in human resources? If so, there is a professional society, the Society for Human Resource Management (SHRM), that produces a vast amount of training and information through its website and magazine. Most professions have websites and related organizations that produce educational material. Interested in becoming a roughneck and working on oil rigs? There are a number of safety- and other industry-oriented magazines, blogs, and other sources of information and training in such an area of interest. Professional organizations are not just for those interested in management positions. Such sources exist for the development of everyone in a particular area of interest. Find out what they are for your areas of interest and start educating yourself. Learn the language of a profession by reading its literature.

We live in an age where the information you seek is available at your fingertips. Use search engines to ask questions and run searches for tips and clues to what you need to know. Ask others in the industry. Leverage your network to reach out to them and learn.

THREAT #6: CIVILIAN MISPERCEPTIONS AND STEREOTYPES

In general, civilians have great respect for what you have done through service to your country. That does not mean that they understand you. Nor does it mean that everyone you encounter in your new career will welcome you with open arms. Some will misunderstand or even fear you.

Today, the unemployment rates among veterans exceed overall unemployment rates. One of the top-cited reasons, which we will address in turn, includes a difficulty in translating military skills into civilian skills that human resources (HR) and hiring managers can understand. Another is the manner in which those skills are identified, the infamous applicant tracking systems (ATSs), software systems that have replaced human judgment when it comes to assessing the skills and fit of all applicants. Beyond these things, there can be other fears and misperceptions that work against you.

At a recent human resources conference, a discussion leader raised an important question: Why do you not hire more veterans? The discussion started out with the typical threats we outlined above. Then the courageous discussion leader asked a difficult question. She asked, "Are you concerned about post-traumatic stress?" A few sheepishly raised their hands, nervous to admit their concern. More and more hands began to go up as the conference attendees saw that they were not alone in their worry about the effects of post-traumatic stress (PTS). That story proves what few want to discuss, that fears of PTS do, in fact, affect hiring decisions for veterans.

This is certainly front-of-mind for many employers, so if you feel there is concern, we recommend you hit it head on by stating, "I know people have concerns about PTS, and I can assure you from a medical standpoint that's not something I've had to deal with."

There is also a degree of stereotyping that takes place among civilians that you may encounter. We have spoken with several veterans who have had experiences similar to the following: A former NCO is hired into a management position with several individuals who have been with the company for many years, have had no previous exposure to military leaders, and have worked under conditions of low morale and poor results for some time. The employees are told by senior managers that a former military leader has been hired to get their department back in shape. Put yourself in the position of your new direct reports. They are already tired and fed up with the company or their previous boss, they are close to walking out for good, and they are told that a veteran is coming in to fix things. Imagine their thoughts of a boot-camp-style manager.

In one instance, a newly hired veteran was met with a very cold reception from his new team. The fear and apprehension was palpable. The veteran had no idea what his team had been through under the leadership of an incompetent and abusive predecessor. Not more than a year later, after a complete turn-around in productivity and morale, the predecessor came back to visit the offices. The bad memories returned to the team. Right after that visitor left, one of the senior members of the team approached their veteran boss and said, "You have no idea how scared we all were when we heard that some former military person was coming in to get our department straightened out. I was ready to quit. But you saved us. Thank you!" The style of good leadership that veterans bring to civilian businesses is often overlooked.

Be conscious of these stereotypes and misperceptions. In the end you will prove them wrong, but they can present obstacles to success as you make your transition into your first civilian career position.

THREAT #7: RESUMES

We predict that resumes will eventually become relics of the past, but for now they are still important parts of the hiring process. You need to have a resume, and it needs to be done well. If you have been paying attention to what we have said about translating your military skills into civilian terms, the resume is where you need to spend effort doing so. Appendix D provides guidance on the proper structure of a resume, as well as some tips. You can also pay for professional resume-writing services and get some assistance from your local transition workshops and programs. We have seen some professional services offered for free to veterans as well. So, check into what is currently available through the transition services organizations at your base or installation.

We will, however, provide some broad guidance that you may or may not get from other sources or services. Word is getting out that you must translate your military experience into a language that is comprehensible to civilian HR and hiring managers, but there are still many veterans who have not received this important advice. We reiterate it here: Your resume can be a threat to landing an important career opportunity if it does not communicate that you would fit well at the hiring company.

One of the greatest threats, however, is not so much the way you describe your skills as in the humility you naturally have in describing your accomplishments. In your military experience, you were probably encouraged not to talk or brag about your accomplishments. This may be especially true if you were part of an elite branch or team.

Perhaps your accomplishments were even classified. That is quite a different attitude from your civilian counterparts. In the civilian world, job hunting is all about self-promotion and you must not be shy about the great things you have done. You must highlight those accomplishments in your resume, and not be afraid to brag a little.

As you develop your resume, keep in mind that civilian employers want to see quantifiable accomplishments. Dig up all your old evaluations, fitness reports, medal commendations, and citations and use the numbers from those documents to add quantifiable accomplishments to you resume. Whenever possible, cite instances where your metrics reflect improvement by a percentage rather than a hard number. Numbers are hard to put into context, whereas percentages tell a clearer story.

Building your resume is going to be a lot easier for you once you have worked through the value proposition and demonstrations of effectiveness exercises that we present in Chapter 8. You will also discover that thoroughly filling out your LinkedIn profile will help identify and clarify some of the things that you should include in your resume.

If you have an opportunity to send a potential employer a cover letter with your resume, do so. A cover letter introduces you to an employer. It may be your first opportunity to sell yourself (refer to Chapter 8) and make a lasting impression. Cover letters are formal business letters of about three paragraphs that establish your interest in a position and why you believe you are qualified. They do not repeat information that is included in your resume.

Refer to Appendix E for a standard cover letter template. The text of a cover letter should follow a three-paragraph format. In the first paragraph, establish how you found out about the position. Hopefully, you heard of the position through someone who knows both you and the hiring manager. Establishing a common connection is a powerful and memorable way to start. It compels the reader to reach out to that common connection to find out more about you.

The second paragraph of a cover letter should explain why you would be a great fit for the position. You should summarize the most significant experiences and skills that qualify you for the job. This second paragraph is your opportunity to use a targeted value proposition. In Chapter 8, we will provide a detailed explanation of how to develop a value proposition.

Finally, you will want to close your cover letter with a paragraph that states your interest and excitement about the potential to work in the advertised position and company. Conclude with a declaration that you would be excited to have the opportunity to meet and discuss your background, then thank the reader for his or her time.

THREAT #8: APPLICANT TRACKING SYSTEMS (ATSS)

Even civilians, and probably many hiring managers, dislike applicant tracking systems. Unfortunately, they are threats you must face. As mentioned earlier, companies use ATSs because of the huge number of applicants that respond to each job posting. It is not uncommon to have hundreds or even thousands of respondents to a single posting. Imagine that you are an HR manager or hiring manager. You are already busy working long hours every day and your staff has been reduced to a small and extremely busy team, with a stack of several hundred resumes to read through to find a few top candidates to call for an interview.

Hiring managers simply do not have time for that. For now, HR departments use ATSs to address this dilemma. If you have any experience applying for job postings, you have probably recognized that many employers require you to either fill out an online application that is much like manually inputting your resume, or they require you to upload a Word document of your resume to an online system. You may think that this spits out a report with all your detailed information directly to the HR or hiring manager, but that is probably not the case. You are most likely uploading your information into an ATS that stores your data with that of an untold number of other applicants. The job that you are applying for may have a description that was designed by the hiring manager, who knows exactly what he or she needs in a good hire. In other cases, an HR manager has done his or her best to translate or describe what the hiring manager wants in terms of skills and experience from an applicant. With all the respondents' information stored in a database, the ATS simply searches for matching key words and language that you used in your uploaded resume or manual responses to questions. If you do not give the ATS the language it is looking for, it will never select your resume as a potential candidate. Regardless of your real qualifications, if the language you use does not match what the ATS is programmed to recognize as a match, no human being will ever see your resume. The ATS is a potential black hole in the employment process—so much so that even many employers are beginning to express frustration.

What hope is there? You can beat the ATS. All you need to have are the language and key words that the HR managers have programmed into the ATS—and finding that can be easier than you think. If you are responding to a job posting, just look at the description of the job that the employer has posted. It is likely that this is the very information that has been programmed into the ATS. You should use that posting as a guide to the language you need to use in your resume.

It will help a great deal if you develop your resume in a way that speaks in the general language of the type of career position that you are looking for. That way, your resume will already be formatted in a way that is friendly to the ATS regardless of which company or specific job posting you are responding to.

For guidance on how to do this, refer to Appendix F, where we will show you a step-by-step method to build the right language into your resume and beat the ATS black hole.

THREAT #9: INTERVIEWS

You have a career plan and you have identified the first job opportunity that aligns with it. You have successfully defeated the ATS, or you have made a personal connection through your professional network that ultimately led to an interview. Unless you had a career before you joined the military, you have probably never had to interview for a job before, so you probably have some anxiety about it. That's okay; some anxiety will feed your desire to do well in that interview.

Between the two of us, we have interviewed hundreds of individuals from entry-level, unskilled labor positions to executive positions. We have both been on the other side of the desk, so to speak, and have been grilled by potential employers for a position we sought. We can tell you that the interview experience is as widely varied as the job market itself. There is no single, common experience. What you experience in interviewing can be unique, or nearly so. You'll probably have some great stories to tell—and, more importantly, you'll learn about the organization you're interviewing with.

Even so, there are some standard formats you should expect. There is the one-on-one interview, where the hiring manager or HR manager sits down with you and asks you questions for about 30 minutes, thanks you for your time, and ends with telling you how or when they might follow up. You might encounter a team interview of two or more managers who take turns asking you questions. You might even encounter a large group or a panel interview. The reality is that if you are being seriously considered for a position, you'll likely have several kinds of interviews. Your interview experience may start with a telephone or video-conference interview with an HR manager that is followed up with a one-on-one, in-person meeting with the hiring manager, followed by a panel interview by the team. If this is the kind of interview structure that you experience, you are in luck because the employer that goes through that kind of trouble really cares about what they do and is making sure that they are making the right hiring decision for you and for everyone on their team.

If you were to go through the interview process here at Afterburner, Inc., you would be in store for something a bit different. You would come in to our corporate office around 1000 hours, receive a tour, meet the entire team, and then meet with Jim, the CEO, shortly thereafter. In that interview, Jim would test your general business knowledge and your knowledge of Afterburner to get a feel for your personality and overall qualifications. Then, you would go to lunch with the senior leadership team, where you would encounter more questions in an informal atmosphere. Finally, you would be given a few minutes to prepare a lesson and teach the Afterburner team. At a predetermined time that afternoon, the entire team would gather in a classroom for your lesson. Afterward, the team would debrief you in great detail on what you did right and what you did wrong. Do you have a thick skin and take criticism well? Finally, you would have the opportunity to debrief the Afterburner team on your interview experience. We show the same deference and respect for criticism from interviewees as we expect them to show us.

In all, an interview at Afterburner takes up the better part of a day for the interviewee and the interviewers. It is an enormous investment in time and effort for us. We take the process very seriously because we must be certain that we are hiring a good fit for our company. Every good hiring manager that you encounter in your career development should have the same level of seriousness about making a hiring decision as we do. That doesn't mean that they should spend a day with you, like we would. It just depends on the context of the position and the company. We are unique, so we do some unique things—many that we won't tell you about.

So, how do you prepare for interviews when their format can vary so widely? Well, it is easier said than done. First, you have to know yourself and your qualifications. Second, you have to know the business that you are interviewing. Yes, you read that right. We said that you have to know the business that *you are interviewing*. Interviewing is like a date. You want to get to know your date, while your date wants to get to know you. Just like a company will select a few finalists to interview and, in the end, pick one, you want to be in the same position with several companies. Best-case scenario, you have several simultaneous offers from which you will choose one. Just like the hiring company, you want to have multiple options so that you can pick the best fit for you. So, if you think that an interview is just a meeting in which you answer questions, you need to expand your scope. An interview is a time for you to ask questions, too. An interview is an opportunity to get to know a potential employer and decide if they fit your career HDD.

Chapter 8 will help you determine your qualifications. It will help you determine your qualifications so that you walk into an interview ready to tackle questions that determine how well you fit. We will help you define those qualifications in terms of the strengths that you have already developed as part of your military experience. Appendix G provides examples of many different questions that an interviewer might ask, as well as tips on how to answer those questions in terms of demonstration of effectiveness. (More on that in Chapter 8.)

Practicing for an interview is essential. We cannot stress this point enough. The best way to prepare is for you to have a friend or colleague come up with a list of questions from the appendices we offer and pretend to be an interviewer. Have them interview you and make that experience as real as possible. Do not look at your notes. Do not ask for a time out. When you can pass a practice interview, you will be ready for the real thing. Record yourself on video to watch your mannerisms and expressions, and adjust to improve your body language. Watching yourself is a powerful means of rapidly improving your skills! Furthermore, it is not a bad idea to apply to some jobs if for no other reason than to practice interviewing in a real setting. There are also professional career coaches that can provide mock interview practice and guidance for you.

Once you know yourself and are ready to interview, we provide several additional appendices to guide you through the research and question-preparation phases for each individual job opportunity. Appendix Q addresses how to generate good questions to ask an interviewer, and Appendix H takes you step by step through how to prepare for an interview. But you have to win that interview first, so before you jump right in to filling out applications and responses to job postings, you need to finish your career planning.

You have your clear career HDD, and we have reviewed some of the common threats that stand in the way of you achieving that career HDD. What other threats stand in your way? These threats can be personal or unique to you. They can be related to the kind of career, the industry, or the profession that interests you. Once you have made note of those additional threats on your worksheet, determine whether they are controllable or uncontrollable. Do not worry about how you are going to negate, mitigate, or avoid those threats just yet. We will address that later. For now it is important to just think of the barriers or challenges that stand between you and your HDD.

Chapter Debrief

- No one achieves anything worthwhile without effort. There are always things that can derail our best efforts. What are the threats, challenges, or obstacles that stand between you and the achievement of your career high-definition destination?
- One of the greatest threats to a rewarding career is a failure to understand your own personality, temperament, likes, and dislikes. Chasing a career that seems interesting can turn out to be a disillusioning experience. Be honest with yourself and get to know yourself before you design your future career.
- Make sure your virtual signature, the information available to anyone who searches for you online, is accurate and represents your qualifications and career intentions accurately.
- Adapt your language, knowledge, and appearance to the context and culture of the company and team you join.
- Be aware of the potential misperceptions that civilians have of you and your service experience. Do not fall into the stereotypes they may expect.
- Take your resume seriously, translate it into a language that civilian employers can understand, and include quantifiable achievements.
- Understand the threat that applicant tracking systems (ATSs) pose, and counter that threat with a resume that uses key words and language that relates directly to each individual job posting.
- Interviews work both ways: a potential employer assesses your fit within their organization, while you assess the job opportunity's fit within your career HDD.
- Know yourself and your qualifications before you interview. Practice interviewing.

CHAPTER 5

IDENTIFY YOUR RESOURCES

SIX STEPS OF PLANNING

1. Determine the mission objective.
2. Identify the threats.
3. **Identify your resources**.
4. Evaluate lessons learned.
5. Develop a course of action.
6. Plan for contingencies.

Business strategy, like military strategy, requires considerable thought, insight, and decision making. Although business scholars often disagree on how to define strategy, most agree on a single aspect of what strategy requires: the careful application of resources. We believe that strategy is simply expressed as the means, or the path, to achieve your goal. In your case, the goal is your career high-definition destination (HDD). Your path may be straightforward or it may be complex. Regardless, strategy should be expressed simply and in terms of the careful consideration of threats, as we have reviewed in the previous chapter, as well as a careful consideration of resources.

Apple founder Steve Jobs demonstrated the impact of resources on the basic principle of strategy when he said, "I'm as proud of what we don't do as I am of what we do." His was a clear and memorable statement of the significance of resource constraints and intentional decision-making. He understood the value of focus.

You too, must focus your resources on your HDD. Your experience has given you a wealth of strengths, tools, and relationships, but you must employ them wisely, in ways that help you achieve your goals. You also don't have the resources to do everything. As you plan your career, you will most likely have to make tough decisions regarding what you will and will not do. Those decisions should be based upon a careful analysis of threats and resources.

We have provided you with some of the common threats that veterans face as they plan and develop their civilian careers. Now let's address the common resources that you may have at your disposal and those you may need to acquire. As you consider these resources, keep in mind that, in a perfect world, you would want to identify resources that will negate, mitigate, or avoid the threats that you have identified. It's tempting to get focused on matching specific resources to specific threats, but that is a trap. It is useful to do that to an extent, but remember that your career HDD is not to eliminate threats. Focusing on that would be the equivalent to fighting every battle and every enemy combatant—it doesn't necessarily win the war. Instead, your focus should be on achieving the objective, rather than eliminating the threats. It is a fine distinction but a very important one. So, when assessing your available or needed resources, ask, "What resources do I have or need to achieve the HDD?" If you are familiar with planning in combat arms, you are basically asking yourself, "What are my *force multipliers*?" Following are some of the common resources you should consider.

VETERANS' BENEFITS

You may be retiring from military service. That means you should have a secure source of income and a host of other benefits. We recognize that your retired pay may not be enough to sustain you at the level you have grown accustomed to, and you are most likely still young with several decades before you can consider fully retiring. Your retirement benefits are valuable resources, but they do not necessarily confer the ability to retire completely.

We encourage you to think about military retirement in its proper context. Military service is a temporary career, and a fair percentage of those who pursue it stick with it for the 20 years it takes to earn a retirement. For those who have received their notification of eligibility (NOE) to receive retired pay, read what it says. It states that "eligibility may not be denied or revoked … unless it resulted directly from the fraud or misrepresentation of the person." That's a powerful statement by the U.S. federal government. We live in a time of severe budget deficits and financial uncertainty as the U.S. population grows older, putting greater pressure on the Social Security system. We all wonder if Social Security will be there for us when we grow old. Few companies offer retirement pensions anymore. Most have moved to 401(k) programs that are based entirely on the performance of the economy in general. If the economy is good, a 401(k) retirement plan may rapidly increase in value. If the economy sours, many retirees will have to reevaluate their futures. Thankfully, your military retirement benefits are as close to a guaranteed income as anyone gets—but nothing is ever certain.

The earlier in your military career that you can recognize the fundamental reality that all employment is temporary, the better you can plan, and the more successful you will be in your inevitable transition. The benefits that you receive during and at the end of your military career should be a component of your career and retirement planning. The relative certainty of continued employment in the military up through the first 20 years is a resource that is often forgotten. It is a level of employment that is generally more secure than employment in a civilian business. Use that current security as a resource of time that you need to plan and execute an eventual transition. Do not plant a tree at the moment you need that tree to bear fruit.

Consider the variety of benefits that you have at your disposal as part of your career plan. Refer to Appendix K for a list of veterans' benefits to consider as resources. You should receive a briefing from your local transition services that will cover these benefits. Those services are resources. Note them in this step of the career-planning process. If you are fortunate to have earned retirement benefits, you will be in a good position when it is time to finally take off the uniform. If not, you must identify what you are likely to need when you leave active duty and plan well in advance of that date exactly what you are going to do to develop your career. Remember, if you had begun planning your career transition when you entered military service, time would have been an abundant resource. How much time do you have now? Are you planting your tree?

LEADERSHIP TRAINING

When you entered military service, you began receiving one of the most important educational and experiential benefits you would receive: leadership training. Even if you have just a few stripes on your sleeve, you have already been provided more leadership training and, more importantly, more leadership experience, than your civilian peers.

There is an impending crisis in businesses today. As the baby-boom generation retires, talented younger leaders must fill the vacuum that their exit creates. The exodus of these seasoned, experienced leaders is already taking its toll on businesses. It is a crisis that human resources (HR) managers and corporate executives are scrambling to address. To deal with this crisis, many companies are turning to leadership development programs (LDPs). Some larger firms have built their own leadership training schools, while others seek external companies to augment their efforts to train leaders. Very few companies have institutionalized leadership development like the U.S. military, however, so consider the leadership schools and even advanced degrees you may have had the opportunity to earn in the military—perhaps at senior NCO academies or war colleges—as valuable resources.

Why does the military have such wonderful formal and experiential leadership training? Because, as indicated by the temporary nature of military employment, it is an organization with an up-or-out culture. Few stay for long in one unit. So, the military must, as it always has, spend a great deal of effort building its leaders from day one and continuously thereafter. The requirement to train for technical expertise was the primary concern in corporate training programs. That is changing. Before the past decade, companies rarely invested in their own internal leader development programs. Instead, they leveraged institutions like universities or special external programs. A leadership development program is not a response to a crisis in the military. It's just business as usual. Your formal leadership training is a tremendous resource for you and your future employer. Make sure that you highlight your formal training and leadership experiences in your resume, social networking profiles, and in communications with potential employers. For example, junior enlisted may have completed introductory leadership courses such as the Petty Officer Selectee Leader Course (POSLC), which is required for sailors upon promotion to E-4. Service in any leadership title such as fire team leader or squad leader are significant experiences to highlight. You do not have to be a graduate of a senior enlisted academy or have a certificate from an officer leadership program to have formal leadership training.

Your leadership skills are just what employers need in order to address the leadership exodus crisis. This is especially true if you are in your twenties. Your peers in the millennial generation are generally considered by employers to lack leadership ability and have unreasonably high career expectations. Millennials are perceived to be spoiled and possess an irrationally high expectation for success and recognition in their early careers. Whether that is true or not is irrelevant. Perception *is* reality. Many clients that we encounter have this perception, and it is openly discussed in the HR professional community. If you are part of the millennial generation, your military leadership experiences distinguish you above your peers. This is a great strength and resource that you must leverage for success in your future career. If you have opportunities to receive additional formal leadership training before you transition out, take them!

DUAL CAREER OPTION

When we wrote about the security component of your career HDD in Chapter 3, we noted the possibility of hedging as a strategy for long-term security. The objective of hedging is to have a fallback career or occupation—one for which you have sufficient skills and experience to find employment should your primary career choices run into significant challenges. These challenges could arise from the bankruptcy and failure of your employer or, worse, a shift in the market that renders your career skills obsolete.

We encourage you to consider skills that you may have that will enable you to hedge and create greater career stability for yourself. Of those we would like you to heed one important piece of advice: Don't burn your bridges! As you move forward in your post-military career, always maintain a positive record with any employer and leave an employer on the best possible terms. A previous employer is one of your most powerful references, a resource to help you secure new career opportunities. As we indicated, the civilian workplace is one in which all employment is temporary. Employers understand that, more than likely, you will eventually move on to another employer—and your boss will likely face similar career decisions. It may be that you will be peers someday in a different organization. Building positive professional relationships is essential to your future success. Your reputation moves with you. So you will want to cultivate and nurture that reputation.

The same goes for the remaining days of your military career, of course. You may want to consider transitioning from active duty directly into a reserve status so that you can pursue multiple interests— and reserve military service can be a powerful fallback career strategy, a great hedge with generous benefits.

NETWORKING, MENTORS, COACHES, AND RECRUITERS

When you first leave active duty, what do you want: a job or a career opportunity? We hope you said a career opportunity. How are you going to get that first opportunity? You may get it by searching through job postings and responding to many of them, but, if you are truly interested in developing a career, you need to consider the much more effective means of landing the right career position for you and your career HDD. More and more, people are finding the best career opportunities by networking.

So, let's start by discussing networking in general, and then some of the particular resources that you can develop as a result of good networking. The reality in the employment world today is that the career positions that are most valued are not filled through job postings and career fairs. They are discovered through networks, one of your most valuable resources in the career search.

Stop and think for a moment about one of the most valuable commodities in any organization, whether it is a business or the military. That commodity is trust. People who trust each other are able to work together with much less friction. Things get done, and they get done right. Employees enjoy a trusting environment. High-performing teams are built on trust. Put yourself in the position of a hiring manager. You have to fill a position, it could be an entry-level position or a high-level management position. What is the easiest way to fill a position if there are no internal candidates that are interested or qualified? It's simply this, you ask your peers, your bosses, and even your direct reports if they know anyone with the skill sets you are looking for. In today's world of lightning-fast communications and social networks, you can find candidates very quickly. And, what's more, because those candidates' professional qualifications and personalities are known by people close to you, they bring some level of trustworthiness simply through their close association with your personal and professional network.

One air force veteran found a job in which he made entry-level hiring decisions. He found it difficult to fill positions with candidates that would ultimately be good fits for the company, however. He soon discovered that one of the best hiring strategies was to ask the best employees for referrals. Did they know anyone who they thought would be a good fit for the same job? Anyone who would make a good teammate? Soon, the workforce itself became a successful recruiting force. Retention and performance improved while the time and effort required to identify and hire talent went down.

More and more companies are beginning to see the wisdom in this approach, although many organizations are required by policy to post job openings online or in newspapers. This means that you will have less success responding to public ads as social networking continues to grow in usefulness as a recruiting tool.

LinkedIn is a must for career development. As we write this, there are no other sites that are being followed as closely by career advisors, coaches, recruiters, and HR managers. According to a recent *Fortune* magazine article, 88 of the 100 largest U.S. companies are licensed to use LinkedIn as a recruiting tool.[1] But remember that social networking entirely through virtual space is not enough. LinkedIn and sites like it are simply tools to manage your real networking activity, but they can be very powerful tools. You have to actually go out, shake hands, and have conversations with people that work within the industries, companies, and professions that relate to your career HDD.

Your military service has handicapped you to some degree in your ability to build and nurture networks. This handicap has been recognized, and a few enterprising veterans have launched a social networking site explicitly designed for active and reserve military personnel to begin to manage their professional military networks in the way that civilians use LinkedIn. The site is called RallyPoint, and it promises to help grow your network both inside and outside the military—and ultimately aid in your transition from active duty to a civilian career. It is still a start-up and its ultimate success remains to be seen. Both RallyPoint and LinkedIn are free, so we encourage you to sign up for both.

Networking is how business is done. Sure, businesses market their products, but the real work in business is done through relationship-building. You probably have not put a good deal of focus on building relationships and forming a professional network in order to succeed in your military career. Sure, if you are at the highest levels of leadership in the military, you have most certainly formed good relationships with

---

[1] Jessi Hempel. "LinkedIn: How It's Changing Business (And How To Make It Work For You)." *Fortune* magazine, 168:1, July 2013, 70.

others and networked, but this is generally looked upon with disdain
by the rank-and-file members of the service. We have a derogatory
term for it: *playing politics*.

As you transition into a civilian career, you are going to have to
look at networking and relationship building in a more positive light
because it's how things get done. Take networks out of the human
equation and you get paralytic bureaucracy. The military services are
large and can both tolerate and benefit from a significant degree of
bureaucracy. But for many businesses, bureaucracy is a cancer that
consumes efficiency. Just as companies rely on trust to increase effectiveness internally, networking and relationship building is essential
for companies to flourish in their market. If you fall squarely into the
relator/idealist quadrant of the personality and temperament model in
Chapter 3, you must recognize this weakness and take positive steps
to engage with others on a regular basis. Your future career depends
upon building relationships with others.

If you have ever heard of the six degrees of separation, you are
aware of the theory that everyone on this planet is no more than six
introductions away from any other person on the planet. For master
relationship builders, those six degrees of separation might only be
about three or four degrees. People who can orchestrate large networks have a clearer and easier path to wherever they want to go.
They just pick up the phone, call a buddy, and ask a favor or introduction. And, oftentimes, *just like that*, a business deal is hatched or a
new employee comes on board.

In the career development arena, networking is becoming the way
to do business. The tax and accounting services firm Ernst and Young
is ranked annually as one of the best companies to work for by *Fortune*
magazine. It is aggressively driving employee referrals for new hires.
Ernst and Young reported that employee referrals accounted for 45
percent of non–entry-level newly hired personnel as of January 2013.[2]
Many other major employers are following suit. They've learned that

---

[2]Nelson D. Schwartz. "In Hiring, a Friend in Need Is a Prospect, Indeed." *New
York Times,* January 27, 2013.

the network of people that originates within an organization is the best place to start when searching for new talent. So, if you are not getting connected—if you are not building relationships with others in your chosen career field and developing a professional network—you are missing one of the greatest resources you can have. The career opportunity that you want is more and more likely to be open to you if you know someone on the inside, or at least know someone who knows someone on the inside.

So, how do you start networking? Well, take a look at your career HDD and ask yourself, who can help me get there? What type of professionals with a similar career path would be able to guide me and provide valuable lessons learned? That may still be a tough question for you to answer. The way that you get started is by researching the company or the professional organizations related to your interests. For example, if you are interested in human resources, you need to join the Society for Human Resources Managers (SHRM) and attend their conventions and seminars. You'll find a small army of people who would love to provide guidance to you. Do you want to work in small arms manufacturing? Then you need to go to the annual Shot Show, which is usually held in Las Vegas. You'll find a vast array of professionals from every aspect of the small arms industry.

We warn you to network valuably. Do not go out and search for social and professional organizations to sign up for just for the sake of networking. We are suggesting you network strategically, not ask everyone you shake hands with for a job.

Our advice to you is to become a participating member in related organizations, meet people, learn from what they have to say but don't tell them you are looking for a job. These could be professional associations or perhaps a trade union. Become engaged in networks that interest you and to which you can contribute. Engagement is very important in networking. There's a big difference between a bunch of people that know your name and a few people that know who you are and what value you can bring. The more interested you are in an organization, the more engaged you will be and the easier it is to network—and network valuably!

Nobody would have the time to be meaningfully involved in all the professional associations and societies in his or her particular industry. Stay focused on a few professional organizations most valuable to you. In networking, quality is more important than quantity. Meaningful professional relationships are more valuable than amassing hundreds of social connections.

So, there you are, standing at a professional convention in a sea of people. Some may be like you, while others may be executives or hiring managers. There are those who were once in a position like you and now may even hold the career position that you want. What are you going to do? Well, the first thing you should do is introduce yourself as a military veteran who is interested in whatever it is that aligns with your career HDD. Have a short, introductory conversation, paying careful respect to the particular individual's time, and then invite them to have a more in-depth, one-on-one conversation at another, more convenient time. One of the most effective things you can do is invite them to lunch. Sure, you'll have to buy them lunch, but they will be able to offer valuable advice on how best to pursue your career. Whatever you do, do not ask them for a job. Being that bold will turn most people off, and you will get nothing from them, not even good advice.

What you are doing is asking them to be a mentor. Most people will be flattered that you are asking for their advice, particularly as a veteran getting ready to transition off active duty. By and large, you are viewed as a hero, and an opportunity to help you is humbling to many. We have met with many veterans who have used this basic networking tactic. Not a single one was ever turned down for a mentoring lunch meeting. If you think that such meetings are a waste of your time, you are dead wrong. You are not just broadcasting your career intentions into a vast network as a shotgun tactic, but specifically targeting the right organization and the best people you have access to. You've heard that hope is not a strategy, but serendipity is. Opportunity often arises at moments you least expect it.

Serendipity happens every day in business and the personal relations between people. To illustrate, a high-level executive who had never served in the military but who had recently been inspired by stories from his grandfather, who served in World War II, decided that he would apply for a commission as an HR officer in the U.S. Navy Reserve. He had a conversation with a recruiter and had filled out most of the application that lay on the corner of his desk, unsigned. He had not made a final decision. He received a note from his boss to meet with some training consultants from a local firm. He made the appointment for a week later. When the time for the appointment with the consultants came, the application still lay untouched on the corner of his desk. He greeted the two consultants as they came in for a meeting. He learned that they were both reservists and that one was a Navy Reserve HR officer, one of just a handful of senior officers in a metropolitan area of over 5 million people. Through a serendipitous and totally unrelated twist of fate, that executive was introduced to a potential mentor for a new career. Serendipity happens every day. We cannot count on both hands the number of times such a seemingly miraculous event has happened to us personally. When opportunity comes knocking, open the door—but you don't wait for it to find you. The larger your network, the more you interact with others and build relationships in every aspect of your life, the more likely those serendipitous events are to occur. You increase your chances with every new relationship you initiate.

There are two types of people who can directly help you in developing your career: mentors and coaches. Both are discovered through networking. What's the difference between a mentor and a coach? You should have many mentors, and most will help provide valuable guidance in some single aspect of your career and life. For example, you may have a few mentors in senior management or executive positions in your company that provide advice in selecting the types of positions you should seek out to develop yourself into an executive position later in your career. You may have other mentors who are industry experts working at different companies. You may have spiritual mentors outside of your work life. Mentors can change as your interests change and you progress in your career. Mentors are simply people who have knowledge and experience that can help you along in life. The best mentors understand your goals, so share your career HDD with those you view as mentors. They will be able to guide you best when they understand where you are going.

Coaching, on the other hand, tends to be a more formal exchange. Just like a coach on a sports team, a coach is appointed or established through some professional relationship. There are many different kinds of coaches and some become coaches through specialized training and certification. There are executive or leadership coaches that assist business managers and executives in improving their leadership skills. There are life coaches that specialize in helping people achieve personal goals. There are also career coaches who can help you with many of the subjects in this book. Career coaches will help you set professional goals, develop your resume, work through mock interviews, and even help you in your search for a good career opportunity. Normally, you or your company will hire a coach and pay them. Mentors are free; coaches cost money.

Recruiters are another type of individual that you may identify through networking. Recruiters are professionals in the career placement industry that match people to jobs. Recruiters usually work to place professionals in a specific industry or with a specific skill set. For instance, there are recruiters who specialize in placing military veterans in the defense-related industry. The best advice that we can give you is to ask around and do some research to find out who the best recruiters are in the industry that relates to your specific career HDD.

A good recruiter will use a process that makes them proficient and successful. A good recruiter will ask a lot of questions and speak with you multiple times before submitting you for a particular opportunity. A good recruiter will always be honest and deliver the truth, good or bad. He or she will provide honest feedback, regardless of the circumstances, to help you if a position is not a good fit. Recruiters will have visited the client to understand more about the company's culture, environment, and needs, and will never send your information to another client without your approval. They'll take phone calls around the clock, be responsive to you, follow up within 24 hours, and prepare you for an interview by providing important intelligence about the role. After an interview, they'll follow up with you and the client. Overall, recruiters take the time to understand your personal background and motivations to help you find a good career fit. A good recruiter should also ask you hard questions such as:

What is your current salary?

Have you ever been terminated from a position?

Will you be able to return calls and e-mails within 24 hours?

Have you had any interviews recently?

Finally, a good recruiter will not try to force you into a position that does not interest you. He or she will do everything possible to make a good fit for both you and the employer.

If you decide to work with a recruiter, work with one who has recommendations from people in your network, and has been in the business for a few years. Then, ask them if they work on a retained or contingency basis. The best case is to work with a recruiter on a retained basis. This means that a company or several companies retain that recruiter's services because they trust them to place good employees. That does not necessarily mean that a recruiter who works on a contingency basis is not a good recruiter, because many companies prohibit retaining recruiters, which forces them to work on a contingency or job-to-job contractual basis. But if you find a recruiter who has good recommendations, has been in business for many years, and works on a retained basis, chances are you are working with a good one. The best ones are not only resources for finding that first career opportunity, but good recruiters can also be career-long resources that help you move from opportunity to opportunity, accelerating you toward your career HDD. Just one last piece of advice regarding recruiters: Never pay a recruiter. Recruiters are paid by the hiring companies rather than the people they place. If you encounter a recruiter who wants a fee from you, walk away.

There are many resources available to you from a variety of government and private companies and individuals. They may be transition and employment services, military and VA benefits, scholarships, information available on a multitude of websites and printed materials, local civic and church organizations, and even family and friends. What resources are available to you? What resources do you need to achieve your HDD and negate, mitigate, or avoid the threats you have identified that stand in the way of you and career goals? Take some time to make of list of those resources and write them down in Appendix B. Take some more time to search for additional resources. These are important activities as you embark on a new career, but we believe that building a professional network that can provide you with guidance and opportunity for many years to come is potentially one of your greatest resources. The beauty of a strong professional network is that you are not the only one who benefits from it. Everyone benefits from it. You have to help others, too.

CHAPTER DEBRIEF

- Plan early in your military career for its ultimate termination, and realize that most employment is temporary.
- Utilize your veterans' benefits. Get counseling from the various programs and transition services at your local military base. Make a list of those benefits.
- Leverage your leadership training and experiences because these skills distinguish you from most of your civilian peers. Seek out formal leadership training opportunities in the remaining time you have on active duty.
- Consider reserve military or National Guard service as a second career option to continue gaining valuable experience and provide additional employment security in your career.
- Build and nurture a large professional and personal network that can supply you with advice and opportunity. Leverage serendipity—the more people you know and interact with, the more likely great opportunities will arise.

(continued)

(continued)
- Seek out many mentors to help advise you on the right course to your career HDD.
- Be careful in selecting a recruiter if you choose to do so. Never pay a recruiter.
- Make sure you create a LinkedIn profile and use the site to manage your network.

CHAPTER 6

EVALUATE LESSONS LEARNED

SIX STEPS OF PLANNING

1. Determine the mission objective.
2. Identify the threats.
3. Identify your available and needed resources.
4. **Evaluate lessons learned**.
5. Develop a course of action.
6. Plan for contingencies.

Everyone thinks that they plan well. In truth, some do and some don't. Some people may even take the time to brief what they plan, but one thing is for sure: Everyone executes, some more effectively than others. However, few debrief, or conduct some form of formal learning activity at the end of a project or mission. It doesn't matter whether you call it debriefing, after-action review (AAR), or postmortem, the point of learning from what you execute is to produce a *lesson learned*. It's your opportunity to recognize what you should or shouldn't do in the future. Civilian businesses have recognized the value of debriefing practices, but reading about how to debrief or conduct an AAR and actually facilitating one are two very different things. Hence, teaching teams how to debrief and produce lessons learned is vitally important. Debriefing is another rare skill that employers need. You must help them recognize this.

Military teams conduct formal learning processes to identify lessons learned. Once documented, teams utilize those lessons in future planning. This simple approach to planning, then executing, then learning, then planning again creates a powerful cycle of continuous improvement. Step Four in the planning process, then, is the point where we take a look at those lessons learned and evaluate which ones may be beneficial to our individual career plan.

First question: If you have never embarked upon a career outside the military, where do you find the lessons learned? Ask your network. This is why the network is so important. You might ask your network if you need a master's degree to be successful in your chosen career. If so, in what area should you earn your degree? The common perception is that master's degrees are a good thing and that you should get one if you want to be a manager or, eventually, an executive. But this is not necessarily true. Before you decide to invest the time and money in a master's program, you should use your network to guide you. There are many people employed in entry-level positions right now that have master's degrees who report to people with only bachelor's degrees or no degrees at all. You need to seek out mentors and other professional sources to help guide you on the right educational path to get the right degree, if any, at the right time. Making assumptions can waste the two most valuable resources you may have: time and money. In the remainder of this chapter, we will provide some general lessons learned for you to consider as you build your own career plan.

TRANSLATING JOB TITLES

We have noted at several points in this book the necessity of translating your skills into language prospective employers will understand. First, you'll need to translate your job title into something recognizable. For junior enlisted, you will probably want to use job titles that reflect your technical expertise, or that imply a level of responsibility such as coordinator or specialist. For example, if you work in supply and logistics, an appropriate title might be logistics coordinator.

For mid-grade enlisted, non-commissioned officers (NCOs), and some junior officers, your titles should communicate that you have leadership experience. A sergeant or petty officer might legitimately use the title supervisor, or even manager, whereas a captain (O-3) might also use manager or even director to describe his or her scope of responsibility. (Note that in Europe, director often means CEO.)

Among higher ranks, there is a tendency to equate the highest levels of responsibility with its direct correlation in civilian business. The highest level of authority in business is the chief executive officer, or CEO. It is more than a stretch to suggest that any military officer, regardless of rank and scope of responsibility, has the requisite experience that is equivalent to a CEO. Military officers do not report to stockholders or boards of directors. They are not responsible for revenue. They may have leadership experiences that surpass those of any CEO, but even the highest levels of responsibility in military services do not confer business management experience.

We suggest several options to translate your title into something more appropriate in civilian business. For any officer who has held a command position with UCMJ Article 15 powers, we suggest that you use the title general manager. Just like the scope of responsibility for command positions, a general manager might have responsibility for a retail store with a few dozen employees and a small budget, a large multistory department store with hundreds of employees and millions of dollars in budgets and revenue, or a huge industrial plant that employs thousands and produces hundreds of millions of dollars in products annually.

Another title worth considering is chief operating officer, or COO. For a company, a COO usually holds the next-most-senior position to the CEO. Functionally, a COO serves in a capacity similar to the S-3, N-3, J-3, G-3, and so on in the standard military organization. So, for officers who have served in such staff positions or as executive officers, use of the title chief operating officer is not a bad choice for translation.

The senior enlisted titles are a bit more challenging to translate because the position and scope of responsibility of an E-7 to E-9 and the vast responsibilities of someone serving as a command sergeant major or a force master chief petty officer are clearly executive-level positions. It's just that civilian companies do not generally have something similar. However, titles like director or even executive director may be appropriate.

RESEARCHING THE OPPORTUNITY AND THE COMPANY

Another important lesson learned is to do thorough research on the industry in general, and the company in particular for which you wish to work. Most hiring managers want to hire someone who shows enthusiasm for their company. There is no better way to do this than to demonstrate a thorough knowledge of the company by referencing relevant facts in your answers and asking intelligent questions.

Start by going to the interviewing company's website. Most companies will have an "About Us" tab. You will want to read all the pages under that tab thoroughly and take notes. There are a few very rich sources of information that you will probably find on such pages. The first is a page containing press releases. Press releases will give you great insight into current events within the company and build a good level of situational awareness around the company's operations. You will also get a sense of the company's success and stability in its market while learning some of their language and lingo. Another very important source of information is the annual report that all publicly traded companies are required by law to publish. These reports are usually introduced by a written statement from the CEO that explains the challenges of the market and the primary strategies that the company plans to employ in the following year. These reports provide a wealth of information, both quantitative and qualitative.

One way to impress a potential employer in the interview process is to explain that you are a customer and demonstrate knowledge of their product line. This is not always possible, of course, because not every business sells a product or a service directly to consumers. Even if you are not a direct consumer, consider what products and services that you may have used in your military service that the company may have provided through government contract. If you do not know, do some research online to see if the company holds any government contracts. Having such a high level of product awareness will impress employers. Such knowledge can distinguish you from other candidates and possibly make the difference between an offer and a pass. You will also understand where their company is in its life cycle, and how to align your experiences into the position that is being offered.

The bottom line is that if it is reasonable for you to have knowledge of a company's products and services, you had better be able to speak positively of those products and services. Showing no interest in the value a company provides its customers will clearly indicate to a hiring manager that you are looking for a paycheck, not a career.

CONSIDER TIMING

How important is timing to you? Do you intend to leave active duty one day and start a new job the next? Are you planning to start your job search after you leave active duty or at the start of a terminal leave period? Timing can be tricky, and you need to consider how long it will take you to find the right opportunities, secure a job offer, and then set your start date.

At present, the average civilian takes four months to a year to find a job. Because that range is so wide and it takes into consideration everyone in the workforce, it provides poor guidance for you to plan your transition. Those average times depend upon the industry and profession. Civilians do not face the same fundamental challenge as you: In the military, you do not have the opportunity to look for a job, accept an offer, and then turn in a two-week notice. You will most likely have to determine a specific date to end your active military service if you even have a choice in the matter. Military service forces you to put all your career cards on the table. Civilian employment allows you to play those cards close to your vest.

As you develop your career course of action, consider that the minimum time required between the time you accept a job offer and you start work is about two weeks. Jobs that are seasonal employment or minimum wage can be shorter than two weeks. But most other jobs will require a series of additional requirements before you are officially hired and start to work. You will most likely be given a contingent offer, meaning that the company is offering to hire you so long as certain conditions are met. Common conditions include background checks and drug tests. Furthermore, once you start a new job, you won't likely get a paycheck for at least two weeks because most companies process payroll only every two weeks or twice a month. The bottom line is that you should expect a month between your acceptance of a new job and your first paycheck.

If you are looking for a management or highly skilled technical position, then you want to be ready to identify opportunities and execute to secure them about 90 days prior to terminal leave or actual separation. You will need that 90-day window because higher-level positions will have much longer hiring cycles than hourly and entry-level positions. Months can pass from the time a position is posted to the time the applications are closed and interviews are conducted. Most of those cycles do not exceed 90 days. Unfortunately for you, if you identify an opportunity more than 90 days before your actual release date, you won't be able to accept it because the military will not let you go early.

You should also consider that it is unlikely that you will secure a job offer between late November and the first few weeks of January. During the holiday season, businesses do not put much effort into filling positions because of the disruptions of so many vacations. Hiring managers and other decision makers have a hard time getting together to discuss a new hire and arrange interviews. Of course, if you want a part-time job in retail, early November is the time to look because that is gift-shopping season when retail stores make a huge portion of their annual revenue. So, they augment their workforce with part-time employees.

PLAY THE FIELD

Moving on, another important lesson learned is to not get dead set on a single job opportunity. You must play the field. You can certainly focus on a particular well-fitting opportunity, but you should not rest all your hopes on it. You want options. As stated before, in the best case, you would get offers from several companies simultaneously, enabling you to cherry pick the one you want most and leverage the other offers to get the best benefits package. The more common experience is that you will get a single offer while simultaneously managing the interview process with other opportunities. So, you may get an offer from one company that you like, but not as much as the opportunity you're waiting to hear about; you'll have to make a choice on whether to take the offer or pass in hopes of a better one. Those are tough decisions, and you want to make sure you are playing the field so that you at least have those options.

ESTABLISH CAREER PROGRESSION

That leads us to another very important lesson regarding something you should not do. You should not take a job, work for a year, take another job with a different company, work for another year, and so on. You do not want to have a resume that suggests that you are indecisive, uncommitted, or simply can't hold a job. One of the first things a hiring manager will look at on your resume is continuity from one job to the next. If the positions held are of short duration and in different companies, they are going to see a big red flag in their head that says "Do Not Hire!" However, if those positions are in the same company and of moderate duration, they will tend to think that you are a high performer that advanced rapidly. Part of your long-term career objective should be to establish a rational civilian career path. The positions you have held, the companies that have employed you, and the duration of each position speak volumes to a hiring manager. The best resumes show that you are progressing along a rational career path without unexplained gaps or sudden changes. Therefore, establishing a career HDD and following an intentional career course will look great on your resume.

GO OR NO-GO

Now that we have introduced some of the common lessons that will help inform you in your career planning process, consider some of the specific lessons learned that affect you in your unique circumstances. Ask people with a military background and career intent similar to yours what they experienced and what they would do differently. We invite you to write them down in your workbook.

Having worked through the first four of the six steps of planning, you have performed a basic risk assessment regarding the achievability of your career HDD. Are you ready to develop the specific courses of action that you will need to take in order to bring your career HDD into reality? In light of the threats, resources, and lessons learned, is your career HDD achievable by the planning horizon you stated? If the answer is yes, great! If the answer is no, then ask yourself what you need to adjust.

Chapter Debrief

- Be careful in translating your military position and titles to civilian ones. Titles should correlate to reflect a similar scope of authority and responsibility. No one should use the title chief executive officer to describe their military experience.
- For an interview, thoroughly research the company and be prepared to ask intelligent questions. Relate positive experiences that you have had with the company's products or services.
- Do not focus on a single opportunity. Cultivate several opportunities at the same time in hopes of receiving multiple offers.
- Pursue a career path that is rational and demonstrates progress in a particular career path. Jumping from job to job indicates a lack of commitment and suitability to a hiring manager.

CHAPTER 7

DEVELOP A COURSE OF ACTION

SIX STEPS OF PLANNING

1. Determine the mission objective.
2. Identify the threats.
3. Identify your resources.
4. Evaluate lessons learned.
5. **Develop a course of action**.
6. Plan for contingencies.

We have reached the point where the rubber meets the road. With all the threats, resources, and lessons learned that you have considered up to this point, it is now time to put it all together into a plan. We call this the *course of action*, but before you get started drafting the specific tasks you will need to take to get to your HDD, take a few minutes to consider how one veteran, Maria, assembled all the separate parts of the planning process together into a seamless whole.

MARIA'S STORY: GETTING STARTED

Before enlisting in the U.S. Army, Maria worked in her parents' paint store on weekends and during the summer for many years in her small town in western North Carolina. It was a family business. She could remember the smell of fresh paint, the ring of the door chime, and her father's belly laughs as he shook hands with dozens of customers every day. She especially remembered the professional painters who would come into the store almost daily to pick up paint and supplies. They usually came in early in the morning or around lunch. Some would even bring their lunch and sit out behind the store on a picnic table with a bright red umbrella that her dad had set up just for them. Her parents would often sit with the painters and let Maria mind the store during those lunch breaks. She worked the front counter and learned firsthand about customer service and building relationships.

At age 18, she joined the army and became a logistics specialist. Twenty years later, she was retiring as an E-7 with a long and successful career behind her. Now what?

Maria's parents had retired from the paint business just a few years earlier and had sold their store. Although Maria loved supply and logistics, for some strange reason, she just liked paint in particular. Maybe it was the scent of it that reminded her of her happy childhood.

Impressed by her logistics knowledge, Maria's parents encouraged her to open her own paint store someday, but Maria knew how much work that was. She didn't want to work seven days a week like her parents. She had her own kids now, and she wanted to spend time with them. She didn't want them to work in a paint store because their mom owned one. She wanted them to have more choices.

Maria loved hanging out in the big home improvement retail stores. She was always planning projects around her own home. She took many of the home improvement classes that they offered on weekends. She would have taken more had she not been working on her degree on weekday evenings. She especially loved painting her kids' rooms. They had grown accustomed to their mom repainting and redecorating their rooms about once every two years—and every time Mom took orders to a new post.

The employees that she interacted with at those big home improvement stores really seemed to enjoy their jobs. They were people like her. Maybe working for a home improvement company was the right career for her, but Maria wanted more than an entry-level position. She wanted to be a senior manager someday. She wasn't sure how she would get there, so she began to ask for advice and to be introduced to managers at her favorite store who might provide some guidance.

One weekend she was able to speak with the store's general manager. She asked about careers in the company. They spoke for well over an hour. Maria was surprised at how much the general manager knew about the company and how excited and open he was to sharing information. "You know, Maria," said the general manager, "after hearing about your interests, and the skills and experiences you have acquired in the army, I think that the position that would ultimately be a great fit for you is a paint merchandiser. A paint merchandiser is responsible for selecting and buying the paint from manufacturers that we sell in the store. It's a very important job that has a big impact on the bottom line for the whole company." The general manager thought for a moment and added, "You know, the paint merchandiser for our company drops by here frequently because we are so close to the corporate headquarters. Let me check into his schedule. Who knows, maybe I can get a face-to-face meeting between the two of you. It's important for merchandisers to speak with customers regularly to get a sense of what products and trends are important to them. You are a great customer, Maria. I think that both of you would benefit from meeting and talking."

And with that, Maria had begun networking into a potential new career. She had met her first mentor, the general manager of her local home improvement store, and, as she would soon learn, the paint merchandiser was due to pay her local store a visit the next month. The general manager set up a meeting and told Maria, "Dave, our paint merchandiser, is really excited to meet you. Come by the store at two o'clock on Tuesday the twelfth to meet him."

The weeks before Maria's meeting with Dave went by quickly. She kept busy in the last weeks of her army career as she prepared for terminal leave and her retirement ceremony. She was expecting a house full of family for the big event, but she still had a little time to spend researching the paint industry. She discovered that there were several professional organizations, even one that posted career opportunities, all over the country. Just looking at those posted jobs helped

Maria realize the vast opportunities that might be open to her in the field. She also found more than a dozen LinkedIn groups dedicated to retail paint sales. She joined them and spent hours learning about the industry by just reading the articles posted in those groups. Of course, there were Facebook groups for painters, too! Maria was learning a lot.

Then, the day came to meet Dave, the paint merchandiser for her favorite home improvement retailer. Dave greeted Maria with a big smile and a vigorous handshake. After some small talk, Maria explained her interests and that she would be retiring from military service very soon. Dave listened intently and asked some specific questions about her professional experiences that included her work in a paint store as a child and her supply and logistics experience in the army.

"Maria, it sounds like you know what you want," said Dave. "You are excited and passionate about it. And, you have some of the fundamental qualifications for what I do as a paint merchandiser. There are many paint merchandisers in the industry, basically any retail company that sells paint would have someone like me on the company's staff. There are many opportunities out there for you. Let me give you some basic guidance on what skills and experiences you'll need to be competitive."

"First," Dave continued, "it's obvious that you are a good communicator and enjoy talking to people. That's a necessity for anyone in this business. Second, you have already begun to learn more about the industry. That shows that you are a go-getter. Frankly I'm impressed by your passion and initiative. You are ready to interview for most entry-level management positions and, perhaps, for some more advanced positions in our company."

"Do you have a degree?" asked Dave.

"No," replied Maria, "but I do have about three years of credit work toward a general business degree. I was planning to enroll in a nearby college once I leave the army and decide where my family and I will settle down."

"That's good," said Dave, relieved. "I don't believe that a degree is really that important, but you are at a competitive disadvantage without one. Our company favors a four-year degree as a basic qualifier for promotion or hiring into the management ranks. The important thing is that you have good oral and written communication skills, and a basic understanding of contracts and administration. Having a background in chemistry is a plus because of the nature of the business. Although, I don't have a formal education in chemistry, some in my profession do. I can tell you that I've learned a lot about chemistry over the years." Dave laughed.

He grew more serious. "Now, let me tell you what most employers will look for as qualifiers to place someone as a paint merchandiser. There are several basic experiences that are common to our position. First, paint merchandisers have experience working in paint stores and selling to both retail customers and to professional painters. It sounds like you have some experience there. But, it has been, what, twenty years since you worked in your parents' store?" Dave asked.

"Yes," replied Maria, "it has been a long time."

Dave nodded. "Well, your experiences are good. They just need to be updated a bit. A lot has changed in the industry in twenty years. A year or so of experience working with customers would help bring you up to date. That doesn't mean you need to work full time in a paint store. You could work part time in the paint department of any of the big retail stores like ours. Maybe you could do that while you finish your degree."

"Oh, yes," exclaimed Maria. "That's what I planned to do for the first year or so after my retirement from the army. I've saved up some money to do that and, with my military retirement benefits to complement the income from a part-time job, my family and I should be in good shape for the next year or two until I can get a full-time management-level job."

"I'm so glad to hear you say that, Maria," Dave said with relief. "I wanted to give you the straight scoop on this industry. I was worried that your expectations might be too high. The fact is that someone with your experience could easily get a management-level position in some companies. But, paint merchandising requires a bit of industry experience that people straight out of the military won't have, regardless of what degrees or rank they might hold. You can't just walk into paint merchandising cold."

"I understand," replied Maria, nodding.

"So, once you get your degree and some experience selling paint to retail and professional customers, you need to get some experience managing a paint department in one of the big retail stores or even managing a small stand-alone paint store. Those sorts of experiences are going to set you up well to take the next step into paint merchandising," Dave summarized, smiling.

Maria began taking notes at this point, outlining the things she needed to do to position herself for her future career.

"Oh, and there's one more important thing," Dave noted, snapping his fingers. "Get some experience with competitors. I've worked for several different companies at some point in my career. It's great to have variety in your experience. Employers see value in that." Dave chuckled, "It's like a little cross-pollination in the industry. It's good for everyone."

Maria thought for a moment. "You mentioned Lowes and Home Depot, Dave. Where are jobs for those companies concentrated?"

"Maria, you're in luck," replied Dave. "You said you wanted to be near your family in North Carolina when you finally found a place to settle, right?"

"Yes, that's right," replied Maria.

"Well," explained Dave, "two of the largest companies are headquartered near that region, with Home Depot's headquarters just a few hours' drive away in Atlanta, Georgia. So, you see, there are enormous opportunities for you in that general area where you can remain just a few hours' drive from your family. And," Dave added, "Atlanta has many good colleges and universities to help you finish that degree."

He stopped for a moment and thought. "You know," he said, "I have a close friend who is a general manager at a store in Atlanta. I don't know if he has any open positions, but I would be happy to recommend you to him."

"Really!?" exclaimed Maria, her eyes widening.

"Oh, absolutely, Maria," said Dave. "You are the kind of employee a store manager would love to have. Let's keep in touch. Here's my card." Dave reached into his jacket pocket and pulled out a business card. "Look me up on LinkedIn and invite me to connect."

"Dave, I can't thank you enough," said Maria. "You've been so helpful. I know what I need to do now, and it doesn't seem nearly as confusing and frightening as it did to me before our discussion. I think I can really start planning some meaningful and important objectives for myself and get moving in the right direction."

"It's been my pleasure," replied Dave. "Don't forget to connect with me on LinkedIn so we can stay in touch."

Dave reached out and shook Maria's hand.

"Oh, and one more thing, Maria," said Dave, smiling, still shaking Maria's hand. "Thank you for your service to our country."

• • •

A few simple conversations with individuals in the industry were all that it took to find the guidance Maria needed. What is Maria's career high-definition destination (HDD)? With what we know of her, it's not too difficult to guess. Perhaps Maria's career HDD looks something like this:

- Planning horizon: Five years from the date of her military retirement.
- Interests and industry: I am a paint merchandiser for a home improvement retail corporation.
- Advancement: I am positioned for further advancement into senior management and, potentially, an executive role.
- Money: I earn a base salary and benefits that are commensurate with industry standards and, combined with my retired military pay and benefits, provide a comfortable living for my family.
- Security: I am employed at a large and profitable corporation in a stable industry.
- People: I work with outgoing people who share my interests. I engage daily with customers and vendors to build lasting business relationships.
- Challenge: I have a challenging job that offers consistent growth opportunities but also allows me to balance work with my life as a mother.

- Location: I live in a suburban area with excellent schools that is no farther than a four-hour drive from my parents. I travel no more than two out of every five days, on average.

The threats unique to Maria's career HDD might look like this:

- Lack of a complete four-year degree.
- No recent experience in paint sales.
- Lack of experience in paint merchandising.
- Retirement benefits not sufficient to support Maria and her family without income supplementation.

Maria has many resources to negate, mitigate, or avoid those threats and help her achieve her career HDD. Those resources are:

- Retirement income
- Montgomery GI Bill
- Military relocation to her home of record or other desired location
- Initial network of mentors in chosen industry
- Professional associations and societies within the paint and home improvement industry
- Social networking sites like LinkedIn and Facebook

Maria has also learned a great deal from her first mentors. The lessons that they provided are invaluable to her career planning. So far, the lessons she has learned are:

- Get up-to-date experience selling to retail customers and professional painters.
- Gain experience running a paint department in a large store or a small stand-alone paint store.
- Gain experience in more than one company.
- Locate near a large home improvement retailer's headquarters within approximately a four-hour drive from the western North Carolina area.

The review of Maria's career HDD and the threats, resources, and lessons learned summarize the first four steps of the six-step planning model we have been following throughout this book. These four steps are not planning per se. That comes next in Step Five. The first steps help us determine exactly what we want to achieve and gather all the information needed.

First, we have assessed how challenging the achievement of our career HDD may be by the planning horizon we chose. Is Maria's career HDD achievable within five years? What about your career HDD? Is it achievable within the planning horizon you selected? If not, do you need to adjust your planning horizon? Or do you need to adjust your career HDD?

Second, the first stage helps us organize all the information that we need in order to actually construct our plan. The first four help us determine the actual tasks, goals, or objectives that we'll need to achieve in order to progress bit by bit toward making our career HDD a reality at our planning horizon. We call that plan the course of action.

THE COURSE OF ACTION

So, what does your career plan look like? It should take a simple form. It should outline what you'll do and when you'll do it. Of course, you can't plan for everything, but you can lay out the primary objectives.

Let's take Maria as an example. She will have some objectives that are unique to her, but she will also have objectives that are common to all veterans. Refer to Figure 7.1 to see what Maria's plan might look like as she puts it together just prior to her retirement.

Notice that Maria's course of action is short and that there are many objectives to achieve in the short term, while there are only a few over the five years of her planning horizon. You will almost certainly have a more detailed plan. But consider that as you work toward your career HDD, you will learn more about how best to achieve it. You should expect to add objectives over the years as you refine your plan and adapt to changes. Your career plan is a living document that you should revisit at frequent intervals in the years to come.

Maria's Course of Action	
Objective / Task	When complete
Research universities in Atlanta, GA, area	May 1, 2014
Gain acceptance to enroll in a university in the Atlanta, GA, area	June 30, 2014
Develop a resume that translates military experiences into civilian business language	June 30, 2014
Have Dave/mentor Red Team my resume	July 15, 2014
Find a home, and relocate to Atlanta, GA, area near enrolled university	July 31, 2014
Identify and join two specific industry associations and societies this year	August 1, 2014
Plan and attend an industry-related tradeshow	August 15, 2014
Secure a part-time position in the paint department at a local home improvement retailer – connect with Dave (mentor) as reference	August 15, 2014
Complete a bachelor's degree in business	December 31, 2015
Secure a management position in retail paint sales at a large home improvement company or small stand-alone paints store	March 31, 2016
Achieve election to senior position in the local chapter of the North American Paint and Coatings Association	January 1, 2019
Secure a paint merchandising position at a large retail company	March 31, 2019

Figure 7.1   Maria's Course of Action

Maria has indicated objectives that address not only the career positions that she should seek, but also her education and networking. She has several objectives that address developing her professional network to include seeking elected office in a professional association. Holding office or some prominent position in a professional society not only helps broaden your network, but also instills confidence in employers that you know your stuff! It's a powerful statement on your resume.

Notice also that each of the objectives within the course of action may require plans unto themselves. Relocating is a tremendous endeavor that requires much planning. Securing a career position requires leveraging both your personal and professional networks as well as job postings that are published through various media.

Interviewing for a specific position requires a plan unto itself. Keep in mind that the planning methodology we have introduced in this book should be used for all the new objectives you might identify in the course of executing toward your career HDD.

As you build your course of action, consider all the common threats, resources, and lessons learned that we have covered in this book. To assist you, we have summarized these items in Appendix M.

RED TEAM YOUR PLAN

Up to this point, you may have planned alone. If so, your course of action is still incomplete. You may know what you want, but how does your plan affect others? What about your family? Did your spouse or children provide any input?

As veterans, we understand the value of planning, and the military developed one of the most powerful tools for improving plans: the Red Team. A Red Team is a group of individuals not involved in a plan's development that is invited to critique or expose the flaws of that plan. The practice of Red Teaming has achieved considerable attention lately. A group of professional Red Team consultants were called in to review and provide criticisms to the ultimately successful raid by U.S. Navy SEALS and U.S. Army Task Force 160 that ended with the capture of Osama Bin Laden. The U.S. Army now offers a rigorous curriculum to train professional Red Team officers at its University of Foreign Military and Cultural Studies.

For a career plan, the Red Team concept is simple. Just brief a family member, friend, mentor, coach, or even your boss on your plan as a whole. Review the career HDD, the threats you have identified, the resources you have at your disposal, the lessons you have learned, and the course of action you have developed. Then stand back and let them provide candid feedback. Is there something you've missed? Is there an action that they may see as ineffective or counterproductive? Be open to criticisms; do not get defensive. Consider their feedback and adjust your plan accordingly, if you agree. Remember that it is *your* career and your plan. You are solely responsible for failure or success.

You may receive conflicting recommendations. So, you will have to be the final decision-maker on what Red Team input your final plan incorporates.

CAREER CONTINGENCY PLANNING

Step Six of our planning methodology addresses contingencies. Because battle plans often fail to survive first contact with the enemy, your military experience may have taught you to include contingencies. When we teach businesses how to plan for the unexpected, we have them determine specific initial actions that could mitigate any of the uncontrollable threats that they identified in Step Two of the planning process. If you identified uncontrollable threats in the exercise we introduced in Chapter 4, now is the time to reconsider what you will do if such threats interfere with your plan. You should also consider other things that can go wrong as you carry out your course of action.

To deal effectively with contingencies, you should set up what we call a "Trigger/Action Matrix." We have provided some examples in Figure 7.2. In these examples, we have indicated the possible contingency in the first block: the clear trigger that will indicate to you that the contingency is occurring, and the actions that you will take to address it. We encourage you to consider contingencies now, as you are making your plan. You should take action in advance of contingencies rather than wait until contingencies force you respond.

Example Trigger/Action Matrix		
Contingency	**Trigger**	**Action**
Too few opportunities aligned with the HDD local to home.	Unable to secure career-oriented position by six months post retirement.	Revise HDD in accordance with new learning, or Identify geography rich in opportunities and relocate.
Unable to secure sufficient MBA funding.	Cost of tuition exceeds 20% of combined retirement and part-time job income.	Secure full-time career-oriented position and pursue part-time MBA/EMBA.

Figure 7.2   Example Trigger/Action Matrix

CHAPTER DEBRIEF

- Consider the threats or challenges that stand in the way of achieving your HDD, the resources you will need to achieve your HDD and overcome the threats, and the lessons mentors and others may provide to you as guidance when developing the course of action (e.g., the individual objectives or tasks you must undertake).
- Utilize the six-step planning process for each objective or task within your course of action.
- Revisit, assess, and revise your course of action at frequent intervals as you learn and adapt to your new career path.
- Red Team your plan. Ask your family, particularly your spouse, to review and provide feedback regarding your plan. Show it to mentors and ask for their critical input.
- Identify uncontrollable threats and other events that may interfere with progress in your career course of action, and create a contingency plan that outlines how you will address them.

CHAPTER 8

SELLING THE MOST IMPORTANT COMMODITY: YOU!

A company's sales force is not the only group of people selling something; everyone is selling something. The cashier at your local grocery store is selling a shopping experience and representing the brand of that particular store. If that cashier checks you through the line expeditiously, asks you for your coupons, inquires if you are a member of the store's loyalty program, smiles and wishes you a good day, then he is probably doing a pretty good job of selling the store's services to you. The store wants you to see value in your shopping experience and come back time and again.

When you wear your uniform in a public place, greet civilians with respect, and respond graciously when they thank you for your service, you are selling the military. You are representing your particular brand, your branch of service. Your behavior encourages others to serve and lets taxpayers know that their government invests their money wisely.

Did you ever defend a position to anyone? Then, you were selling. Sometimes we are successful by selling from an emotional point of view; other occasions call for a rational perspective. If we are expert at selling, we persuade from both perspectives. Regardless, when you argue for an idea, you are attempting to sell it.

You need to view the rest of your career from a sales perspective. You should adopt the perspective that you are, from here forward, selling yourself as a value to a potential employer. And you'll be most successful by leveraging both the emotional and rational aspects of that sale.

In the previous chapter, we saw how Maria won over a general manager and a paint merchandiser. They essentially bought what Maria was selling, but did she convince them to hire her using a rational or emotional perspective? Maria's skills and experiences were not sufficiently developed for her to become a paint merchandiser, so rationally, there is not much to distinguish Maria from a sea of other job candidates. Maria sold herself from a strong emotional position. She exudes excitement and passion—and that's what her employer wanted to see.

To sell yourself effectively, you have to show qualifications and a capacity for engagement. Engagement shows your emotional commitment to your work. To an employer, an engaged employee is a productive and loyal employee; an engaged employee is an asset.

Qualification is the rational component to selling yourself. The capacity for engagement is the emotional component. If you have accurately targeted an interest or industry that you truly believe you would enjoy, and the particular opportunity that you are targeting at any given time aligns with your career HDD, then you should have some real passion and excitement about that opportunity, and a hiring manager will notice.

You want to sell yourself as the best value an employer can get, so think in terms of your value proposition, your rational argument for how you bring value to an employer. It's your sales pitch, so to speak. What will you bring to the job that's unique and that will create value? Because every opportunity is different, you will need to draft or revise your value proposition to fit that particular opportunity.

In this chapter we will lead you through the process of developing your value proposition. A value proposition is not something you sit down and write from scratch. It starts with building blocks that we call *demonstrations of effectiveness*, or DOEs. These DOEs are developed around the LOCKED model that we introduced in the first chapter.

You should have many DOEs. You can summarize those DOEs into a targeted value proposition. You can use DOEs in your resume to highlight your accomplishments. You can put them in your LinkedIn and other social media profiles so that recruiters searching for candidates to fill a position notice your profile. Perhaps most important, your DOEs will provide a list of answers to many interview questions that you'll likely receive. Because you have prepared them thoroughly in advance, you will have the confidence you need when you walk into that interview.

YOUR VALUE ARSENAL—DEMONSTRATIONS OF EFFECTIVENESS

Demonstrations of effectiveness are one- to three-sentence statements that describe a single professional experience. DOEs are packed full of information about your skills and abilities. Here is an example of a DOE from a U.S. Air Force Colonel who applied for and won an executive position as Vice President of Global Diversity and Inclusion at a major medical device manufacturing company:

> Created and executed first-ever Strategic Enrollment Management Plan at United States Air Force Academy, achieving highest SAT and ACT composite scores in history while simultaneously increasing African-American and Hispanic enrollment and graduation rates.

Here is another from a U.S. Marine Corps senior non-commissioned officer:

> Planned and led Force Preservation Program that reduced post-deployment disciplinary issues by 73% within 11 months. Efforts were essential to unit winning top annual award.

Demonstrations of effectiveness are simply stated and direct. These examples look simple enough, but it takes effort to craft them into a clear, concise, and informative structure. It may not appear obvious, but both examples above follow the same three-part structure. Each leads with an action verb that describes the skills you have demonstrated, hence the reason we call them demonstrations of effectiveness.

Following one or two introductory verbs, you should include some descriptive detail that provides some context and scope of the DOE. Finally, end or close the DOE with a quantifiable result. In Figure 8.1 we have dissected the previous examples into these three parts.

If you are having trouble leading your DOE with strong action verbs or thinking through some of the skills and experiences you have had in your military career, consider some of the following: analyzed, built, created, directed, established, increased, organized, planned, and transformed. More good verbs are provided for your consideration in Appendix N.

If you have been studying about interviewing or have been introduced to some interview preparation strategies in transition seminars, you may recognize that the structure of a DOE is similar to the STAR (situation, task, action taken, and result) method for answering behaviorally oriented interview questions. Some additional detail on the STAR method is provided in Appendix E. The DOE, however, provides a compact means of writing and, perhaps, even memorizing the critical information that you need in order to communicate and sell your value to a potential employer. It is easy to elaborate on any given DOE as a response to an interview question by introducing some additional context in accordance with the STAR method. You just have to make sure that you answer the question completely and include the most critical information included in your DOE.

Lead with action	Created and executed . . .	Planned and led . . .
Include detail	. . . first-ever strategic enrollment management plan at United States Air Force academy . . .	. . . Force preservation program that . . .
Close with results	. . . achieving highest SAT and ACT composite scores in history while simultaneously increasing African-American and Hispanic enrollment and graduation rates.	. . . reduced post-deployment disciplinary issues by 73% within 11 months. Efforts were essential to unit winning top annual award.

Figure 8.1   Sample DOEs

As you draft your DOEs, keep in mind that businesses love hard numbers as results. Whenever possible, translate numbers into percentages, such as "improved output by 15 percent." For example, if you were to say that you saved your unit $100,000 in operating costs, that may or may not be impressive to a potential employer. If your unit's operating budget was $1 million, then you have "improved operations budget savings by 10 percent." If the position you are interviewing for manages an operating budget of $500 million, then your meager $100,000 doesn't seem so impressive. You want an interviewer to think, "Wow, if this person could save us 10 percent on our operating budget, that would translate to a savings of $50 million!"

Unfortunately, it is often difficult to translate results into hard numbers. It may also be difficult to translate certain subjective accomplishments into objective results. Try your best and ask for help from others. When you are having trouble quantifying results, you can express the result in terms of a medal or other commendation you may have been awarded. And be sure that you read your medal citations, which often include hard numbers. Citations are a rich source for finding the raw information to construct one or several DOEs. Additionally, pull out all of your evaluations or fitness reports, which provide a wealth of ideas and objective results for drafting your DOE.

If you are transitioning after only a 4-year tour of duty, then you'll have fewer DOEs than, say, a 20-year retiree. So, look very closely at your reports and citations and develop as many DOEs as you can. For those with many more years of service, consider those DOEs that are most recent and most relevant to the post-military career you are seeking. That does not mean that experiences you had early in your career are unimportant. On the contrary, they may have been formative experiences that reveal important qualifications to an employer. However, a 20-year veteran could easily draft several dozen DOEs. Either way, drafting as many DOEs as you reasonably can will help you prepare for interviews.

As you develop your demonstrations of effectiveness, organize them into a structure that best communicates your value to employers. This structure will also help you think through all your possible DOEs in a comprehensive way. That structure is the LOCKED model. Recall that LOCKED stands for leadership, organization, communication, knowledge, experience, and discipline.

L̲OCKED—LEADERSHIP

To develop a leadership-oriented DOE, begin by describing times when you led by example, took responsibility under challenging conditions, and held yourself and your team accountable; established or reinforced standards and processes; cultivated strong situational awareness among your team; facilitated collaboration; empowered others; and developed or engaged your team or subordinates professionally.

Here are some examples of leadership DOEs:

> Directly supervised, trained, and mentored five junior platoon leaders in all aspects of combat, physical, and mental training, resulting in early promotions for three of the five subordinates.

> Led 10,000 soldiers in combat operations, achieving 100% accomplishment of all mission objectives while sustaining zero friendly loss of life.

> Developed and executed mentoring program for 450+ soldiers, resulting in highest reenlistment rate in battalion history, a 75% increase over next-best year.

LO̲CKED—ORGANIZATION

For organizational demonstrations of effectiveness, consider occasions when you established clear goals, measurements, and roles in your team; managed a plan, mission, or project; managed a quality program; utilized process and continuous improvement methods such as Six Sigma, TQM, or Flawless Execution.

Here are some examples of organization DOEs:

> Organized and coordinated the selection, assessment, onboarding, and training of a foreign security force, resulting in 100% transition of operational responsibilities with zero loss of proficiency rating during Operation Iraqi Freedom.

Revamped the Korea-wide supply chain by utilizing Lean Six Sigma methods to efficiently integrate cross-docking with sea, air, and ground transportation, resulting in a 30% reduction in order receipt times.

LOCKED—COMMUNICATION

Communication is an important skill, but one that is often difficult to express in terms of DOE. Consider your verbal and non-verbal communication and writing skills to include documents, proposals, and reports that you authored. Describe customer service experiences, and remember that formal briefing provides excellent communication experience. You may also consider the activities and media you may have used to reinforce and align tactical, strategic, and organizational goals.

Here are some examples of communication DOE:

Led operations and communications center during global military personnel accountability exercise, requiring voice and written reporting to worldwide deployed units. Achieved highest accountability score ever recorded: 99.9%.

Chaired the Sergeants Major Association to create consensus and unity of purpose aligned with the Association's charter, resulting in 100% dues collection and year-over-year membership increase of 40%.

LOCKED—KNOWLEDGE

Knowledge is straightforward, and you should highlight the formal education or training that you have received. Pay particular attention to academic honors and occasions when your personal knowledge contributed to positive organizational results. DOEs in the knowledge category might include professional certifications, organizational learning competencies, or teaching and training skills.

Here are some examples of knowledge DOEs:

Achieved top 20% rating of all leaders enrolled in both primary and secondary leadership development programs.

Consolidated the weapons system training for a 450-soldier department, resulting in selection as the lead facilitator and curriculum designer for the organization's operations readiness center.

Hand-picked to teach datalink programs as an adjunct professor at the Air Force Fighter Weapons School.

LOCKED—EXPERIENCE

Knowledge is a measure of your know-what, while experience is a measure of your know-how. We leave schools with our heads full of knowledge, but using that knowledge to drive positive results is another thing entirely. So, experience is where the rubber meets the road in your demonstrations of effectiveness. It's easy to include other LOCKED values in experience, but these DOEs should concern the jobs and positions that you have held and the scope of your responsibilities. DOEs in this category should demonstrate how you use knowledge and skills to drive results.

Here are some examples of experience DOEs:

Collaboratively developed and secured buy-in for the implementation of a Forward Operating Base land lease in Helmand Province, Afghanistan, by leveraging understanding of strategic partner's cultural components.

Commanded enterprise-level logistics, finance, personnel, policy, and supply chain operations in Iraq, Kuwait, Afghanistan, and Northeast Africa, reducing operational expense by 20% and improving supply chain cycle time by 33%.

Analyzed and solved repair organization's inventory problems regarding overhead costs and parts availability by creating a quantitative analysis program in Excel to provide just-in-time management of parts. Increased parts availability confidence in frontline artisans, curtailed parts hoarding, and reduced wasted labor due to reorder inefficiencies. Projected savings estimated at $100,000+ within 24 months.

LOCKED—DISCIPLINE

For discipline, consider instances in which you have successfully handled stress, task saturation, and significant responsibilities in high-risk environments. You focused on objectives rather than becoming distracted. You accomplished the mission in spite of challenges and distractions.

Here are some examples of discipline DOEs:

Planned and led Force Preservation Program that reduced post-deployment disciplinary issues by 73% within 11 months. Efforts were essential to unit winning top annual award.

Simultaneously led battalion of 450+ personnel forward deployed in a combat zone while also serving as Community Affairs Liaison. Unit awarded prestigious Presidential Unit Citation.

It is beneficial to have a good balance of DOEs from each of the LOCKED categories, but you do not necessarily have to represent all of them. The more variety you are able to develop, however, the easier it will be to respond to interview questions that you may not have anticipated.

DRAFT YOUR TARGETED VALUE PROPOSITION

With a healthy number of demonstrations of effectiveness drafted and a career HDD targeted to a specific set of interests, industry, or even a specific job, you can start drafting your value proposition. You may find it helpful to gather job postings that are similar to the first career opportunity that you seek. The first value proposition that you draft should be general and emphasize words and phrases relevant to the job you're seeking. Refer to Appendix F on how to generate a good list of key words and phrases.

As an example, a navy junior officer leaves active duty after four years and begins seeking a career in operations management in light or heavy industry. The officer drafts the four demonstrations of effectiveness below. Notice that those DOEs that are most relevant to the career path are near the top. Together, they tell a coherent story of one officer's experiences, qualifications, and accomplishments in a short period of time.

Directed and reorganized high-performing engineering team of 140+ personnel through 30% manpower reduction during deployment to a high-tempo operational environment. Maintained refrigeration, air-conditioning, heating, and steam services for an aircraft carrier without fail. Identified as top 10% of officers in competitive class.

Managed ship-wide aircraft carrier ventilation cleaning and maintenance, requiring close coordination and cooperation with 10 separate departments and an ad hoc workforce of 80+ personnel. Efforts commended by ship's captain as superb and having directly contributed to the control and containment of a potentially catastrophic fire.

Planned and executed daily operational activities and ensured safe navigation of a U.S. Navy nuclear-powered aircraft carrier deployed in combat and high-risk humanitarian aid operations. Ship awarded prestigious Meritorious Unit Citation and other efficiency awards.

Analyzed and solved aviation repair organization's inventory problems regarding overhead costs and parts availability by creating a quantitative analysis program in Excel to provide just-in-time management of parts. Increased parts availability confidence in front-line artisans, curtailed parts hoarding, and reduced wasted labor due to reorder inefficiencies. Projected savings estimated at $100,000+ within 24 months. Awarded Navy and Marine Corps Achievement Medal.

In themselves, these sample DOEs are strong qualifiers for someone looking to enter operations management. Notice that this officer used the term "aircraft carrier"; it's safe to say that civilians know what an aircraft carrier is. Civilians will also know what a tank is, but beyond such simplistic concepts you should not expect civilians to understand details and complexities of military operations, weapons, and organizations. So make your DOEs understandable for people without military experience. If you find yourself having to explain what something is, then you should probably phrase it in a different way. If you had to, you could describe an aircraft carrier as "a large aviation support facility for 90+ aircraft." It seems silly, but the burden of translation is your responsibility. Notice that we have left some military terms in our examples, such as "battalion." Civilians will know that a battalion is an organizational unit or will be able to recognize it as such by the context that you use the word; they just won't know the size of that unit. So, these examples let the reader know that it's a unit of 450 soldiers. If you use military terms, make sure that the context leads the reader to understand its meaning.

You should take your DOEs and distill them down to a one-minute value proposition. By one minute we mean that, at a normal pace of speech, you should be able to summarize your value to an employer in about one minute. If you have your one-minute value proposition memorized, you are going to be ready to explain your value to an interviewer and respond to questions such as, "Why do you believe you are qualified for this position?" Below is an example value proposition that we derived from the DOE examples above.

> I am a former U.S. Navy engineering and bridge watch officer who led a large engineering division of over 140 personnel. My division was responsible for the maintenance and repair of a wide variety of equipment such as refrigeration, heating and air conditioning, steam services, hydraulics and elevator equipment, and even washers and dryers. As a bridge watch officer, I had the full trust and confidence of an aircraft carrier's captain to function as his direct representative in daily operations and make decisions in his absence. I have been successful in leading large organizations, providing mechanical services for a crew of nearly 5,000, and coordinating activities in a massive and complex organization. Furthermore, I have applied significant process improvement training to my areas of responsibility that resulted in my earning a Navy Achievement Medal and the personal thanks of my captain for averting a near-catastrophic fire onboard our ship. I believe these skills and experiences are directly relevant to the job as I understand it.

So, what did the officer tell a potential employer in our example value proposition? Look at it one sentence at a time in terms of the LOCKED model.

> I am a former U.S. Navy engineering and bridge watch officer who led a large engineering division of over 140 personnel.

To an employer, the former officer said: "I have relevant *leadership* skills and experience." Now, look at the second sentence.

> My division was responsible for the maintenance and repair of a wide variety of equipment such as refrigeration, heating and air conditioning, steam services, hydraulics and elevator equipment, and even washers and dryers.

In that sentence, the former officer let a potential employer know that "I have *knowledge* of a variety of engineering systems that is relevant to the industry." And, in this case, this sentence implies knowledge of a laundry list of policies, regulations, standards of practice, and safety procedures that are common to anyone working in the industry whether military or civilian. The third sentence says:

As a bridge watch officer, I had the full trust and confidence of an aircraft carrier's captain to function as his direct representative in daily operations and make decisions in his absence.

Now, the value proposition is letting the employer know that "I have *experience* running large organizations." Furthermore, the former officer is letting his audience know that he is trustworthy, responsible, and capable of exercising good judgment. Moving on to the next sentence, we see a summary that re-emphasizes some of the LOCKED categories already mentioned while suggesting another.

I have been successful in leading large organizations, providing mechanical services for a crew of nearly 5,000, and communicating and coordinating activities in a massive and complex organization.

In this sentence, the former officer has told the potential employer that "I have experience in a customer service organization, and I have good communication skills. Furthermore, I can handle a challenge and create success."

The value proposition concludes with an excellent way to respond to a typical interview question. The former officer states, "I believe these skills and experiences are directly relevant to the job as I understand it." When interviewers sit down with you and say, "Tell me about yourself," their intent is not to get you to talk about your favorite color or the pet that you had when you were six. An open-ended question such as "Tell me about yourself" can be a test by an interviewer to see if you have the good judgment to tell them about your professional qualifications. So respond with your value proposition rather than a discourse on your personal interests. When you conclude your value proposition the way that this former officer did, you prompt the interviewer to talk more about the job and the specific qualifications that you have prepared in the course of drafting your DOEs. In other words, you have set the interviewer up to fight on the battlefield of your choosing. You have taken the initiative and turned the focus of the interview toward your strengths.

This example value proposition is just 165 words. You should draft your value proposition at about the same length, between 150 and 180 words. Notice that, in this example, the officer chose to use the phrase "bridge watch officer." That is a phrase that may not have any meaning to a civilian, but this officer explained what the duties of a bridge watch offer were. The difference between a value proposition and a demonstration of effectiveness, besides scope and length, is that the value proposition uses complete sentences and allows for greater explanation of some concepts that you might introduce. DOEs are short and powerful qualifiers, whereas value propositions tell a more complete story. DOEs are great to include on resumes, whereas value propositions can be included as a paragraph in a cover letter.

Once you have crafted a general value proposition, you should review and edit it for each unique career opportunity that you seek. Because every career opportunity is different, you must target your interview preparations. We have already discussed the importance of researching each opportunity. You must also consider the needs of the employer and develop your value proposition to meet those needs. Demonstrate how you are a great fit for the organization. Your ability to communicate your value proposition is critical to your success.

CHAPTER DEBRIEF

- When seeking to secure a career opportunity, you should consider that you are selling your knowledge, skills, and abilities to an employer. To that end, you should express your

(continued)

(continued)

qualifications in terms of a value proposition. The value proposition is your concise sales pitch.

- Before developing a one-minute value proposition, you should carefully consider all your professional experiences and draft demonstrations of effectiveness (DOEs) for each. DOEs provide specific responses to many interview questions and can be used to improve your resume.
- Because every career opportunity is different, you should revise your value proposition to match each unique position.

CHAPTER 9

INTERVIEW TO WIN!

You have worked your personal and professional network and carefully researched job postings that align with your career HDD. You have some interested employers and have been invited for your first interview. What to do now?

Winning the interview is all about organization and preparation. If your military service taught you one thing, it was about preparation and getting organized to execute your mission successfully. Therefore, you must plan for each interview. Luckily, many have gone before you and there is a wealth of experience that can be summarized in this chapter and into a checklist that we have provided in Appendix H.

PREPARING FOR AN INTERVIEW

Research isn't just for companies themselves; you can also research the individuals you'll encounter in the interview process. For instance, an army colonel won an interview with a high-level executive at a large company. The colonel searched the web for the executive's name, and found a goldmine of information on the interviewer and the company, including a magazine article about the very executive he was about to meet. A simple web search can reveal useful information that can set you apart.

Some advice on research can be found in Chapter 6, and we have summarized that advice in the checklist in Appendix H. But there is much more to prepare before an interview, such as practicing your responses to potential interview questions, and generating a list of good things to ask the interviewer. You should find out exactly when and where the interview will take place. That seems simple enough, but you can encounter all sorts of issues if you plan poorly. For instance, will you have to go through security gates at a large corporate campus or at the front entrance to the building? Often, you will encounter both and, if you do, how much time will it take you to get through these checkpoints? What sort of identification will you need? What about traffic? How far do you have to travel to get to the interview location, and what will the impact of traffic be at the time you will be making the transit? If the interview is taking place at an unfamiliar location, you should map it out and drive the route on a day prior to your actual interview. One of the worst things that can happen to you on an interview is for you to show up late.

Showing up late is an automatic disqualifier in the minds of most hiring managers. You should arrive about 10 minutes prior to the scheduled time. This demonstrates good judgment. As a rule of thumb, 10 minutes prior to the prescribed interview time should be your goal. Ten minutes early means that you should be in the office waiting in a chair for the interviewer or HR manager to come for you. That does not mean rolling up to the parking lot of a large corporate campus 10 minutes prior to an interview. Do that, and you will almost certainly be late, as you flail about looking for the right building and floor, and potentially waiting to get through security.

If something truly unforeseeable happens that causes you to be late, communicate the situation to your point of contact.

You do not want to show up too early, either. If you show up 30 minutes early for an interview, you will most likely just annoy the hiring manager, HR representative, or administrative assistant who has to accommodate you and be a good host or hostess until the interviewer is ready for you. Showing up too early can be an indication of poor judgment in the mind of an interviewer.

Treat everyone you meet throughout the course of your interview experience at an employer's offices as if they are the interviewer.

Anyone you interact with can provide feedback to the hiring manager about their experience with you. Some interviewers will judge an interviewee's behavior toward the office's administrative assistants, so be sure always to remain polite and treat everyone with respect.

If you drive to the interview, do not park at the front door, especially if you arrive too early. Being conspicuous in your arrival will offer the interviewer an opportunity to observe you well before the interview starts. Someone from the company may notice you in the parking lot, so ensure your car is clean inside and out; this will help your frame of mind as well. If you're early, be sure not to smoke or loiter before entering the office. Finally, observe office protocols; don't park in a reserved space. Enter the office confidently, but respectfully.

Your personal appearance is also important. We have provided specific guidance about how to dress in Appendices I and J. However, there are two overriding principles to consider when you interview. The first rule of dress and grooming is to be unremarkable. You want to dress well but, at the same time, not draw attention to yourself. You do not want clothing, jewelry, or accessories to distract an interviewer from considering you and your skills. For those of you with lapel pins to signify military medals received, remember that civilians will likely not recognize them, so leave them at home.

The other principle of interview dress and grooming is to dress one level above the dress code of the company. You may read and hear a lot of advice about what to wear to an interview. The standard for men is a dark, solid-color suit. For women it is a solid-color conservative suit and blouse. When in doubt, defer to these standards. However, the working world is highly varied now. Some companies' dress codes are highly informal, so be sure to ask or get a sense of the appropriate attire before you visit the company.

In general, business attire is the default dress described in the appendices. If a company describes its dress code as business casual, then business attire is the next level up. So, in that case you should still dress according to the advice in the appendices. If it describes its dress code as casual, then we suggest you dress in a coordinated jacket and slacks, but no tie.

WHAT TO EXPECT IN AN INTERVIEW

Interview experiences can be as varied as the opportunities you will come across. There are, however, a limited number of types of interviews that you will encounter.

We briefly touched on this earlier, but the most common is the one-on-one interview. It's the kind of interview you probably imagine. It's simply you and an interviewer sitting down in an office or a small conference room. You make introductions and the interviewer asks you questions. This type of interview may be with the hiring manager or with an HR manager.

There is also a panel or team interview. This format is probably utilized more in internal promotions than in interviews with external candidates, but you may encounter them. This will be similar to a one-on-one except that there will be more than one interviewer. It's typically two to four managers that have some shared responsibilities and are vetting a candidate as a team. Some managers like this type of interview because it allows one to sit back and observe a candidate and think about what they are saying a bit more critically rather than thinking about the next question or where to steer the conversation. It can also be a more efficient way for a group of managers or a team to vet a candidate simultaneously and then confer with each other immediately following an interview to reach a panel decision about the quality of the candidate. The drawback is that it can be a bit overwhelming for some interviewees.

Then there is the group interview. A group interview turns the tables: instead of several interviewers interviewing a single candidate, there are several candidates being interviewed simultaneously by a single interviewer. These types of interviews are usually only conducted for entry-level positions where large numbers of candidates need to be vetted. If you find yourself in this situation, you should listen to what other interviewees are saying, and reflect appropriately, adding your own thoughts and experiences. But be warned: You can come across as arrogant and overbearing if you demean other candidates' responses. Instead, introduce your answers with statements such as "So-and-so makes a good point, and I'd like to add that...." Be careful not to insult or demean the other interviewees' comments, because the interviewer may consider that you have poor team skills or empathy for others.

More often, employers are utilizing video teleconferencing to interview potential candidates who are not local to the interviewer. So, be sure you have access to an Internet device with a video camera. This option can provide companies a much more cost-effective means of interviewing candidates, and also help you overcome a distance issue if a potential employer is not willing to pay for your travel expenses to attend an on-site interview. If you do not have the proper equipment at home for this, some document reproduction and shipping stores such as FedEx Office may have video teleconferencing facilities. If a potential employer is willing, you can offer to perform a video tele-conference interview with them. If you have the opportunity for a video interview, review all the instructions and follow directions, dress as you would if it were in person, and look directly at the camera, not at the screen. It is a good idea to record yourself on your own equipment for practice before you perform a live video interview so you can get used to talking into a camera.

Finally, there is the unstructured conversation. At the higher management levels, you are more likely to have what feels like an informal conversation. It may also be the format of a second or third interview. If you have had one or more interviews and you have been called back for an interview like this, you are probably very close to being offered the job. The interviewer is just trying to get to know you and get an idea of who you are and how well you will fit in their organization. They've probably already been sold on your qualifications.

Interviews can also take place outside the office setting. They may take place in a coffee shop or restaurant. This is not unusual and may occur for many reasons. Sometimes, if an employer is getting rid of someone and looking at you as his or her replacement, then they don't want you in the office creating questions such as, "Who is that, and why are they here?"

Employers will often require standardized written assessments and even personality tests prior to an interview. These tests are very common in retail and other frontline customer-service jobs. Don't be surprised if you have to take a written assessment as part of the hiring process. Do not try to game these tests by giving the answer you think that the employer wants to hear. Depending on the level of sophistication, the answers you give on these tests can be cross-referenced to detect deception. Be honest about yourself and the answers you give.

If you appear to be a fit for an employer, then you will likely have more than one interview. The norm is between one and three. Each interview could take the form of any of those we have introduced above. If you are on your third interview, hang in there. You are doing well. Just stick with it and be patient.

INTERVIEW QUESTIONS

In preceding chapters, we have helped you design a value proposition that you should target to each unique career opportunity. That value proposition is a powerful sales pitch that can be used in a cover letter or to answer any one of many introductory questions on an interview such as "Tell me about yourself," or "What brings you here?"

Lou Adler, a recruiting expert, considers one question the greatest of all time: "What single project or task would you consider the most significant accomplishment in your career so far?" We agree with him. If you have developed a series of strong demonstrations of effectiveness, one of those should be the answer to this question. That single project or task can be the starting point for a series of additional questions that dig deeper into why you are so well qualified for the job and what motivates you to do what you do. From the interviewer's perspective, it is going to tell them a lot about what you have actually accomplished and what you deem important.

One of the other great interview questions is "Why do you believe you are qualified for this position?" Another is simply "What brings you here?" The answer to both of these questions is the same. You use your value proposition to answer them. You tell the interviewer what qualifies you for the job and, simultaneously, that the position aligns with your career interests. You saw that the position matched your value proposition and considered that you would be a great fit for the employer. That's why you are there; you're a great value to the employer and the opportunity is a great value to you.

The secret to preparing for interview questions is to know yourself and your qualifications thoroughly. The sample questions that we have provided in Appendix G represent some of the standard questions you might encounter. It also contains some questions that will probe your personality. Chances are that the questions an interviewer will ask will be directed toward your qualifications and experiences. But you have to prepare for a few surprises. We included a few such questions in Appendix G that we have collected from CEOs of large corporations over the years. There are no right or wrong answers. Such questions are revealing tests of character. Just be honest and don't appear shocked when an unexpected or unusual question comes up.

However, there are certain questions that interviewers are legally prevented from asking you. An interviewer should not ask about your age, marital status, religion, health, or family, including your children.

As you answer questions, remain positive in your tone. Never provide negative comments about a previous employer or experience. Interviewers assume that if you will talk about a negative career experience in an interview, then you are far more likely to make negative comments daily and degrade morale or even undermine authority in their business. Also, be cheerful and have a generally positive demeanor, but remain professional.

Don't interrupt or talk over the interviewer. Let them finish their thoughts or questions.

Answer them with an appropriate amount of detail and explanation. Most interviews won't have many "yes" or "no" questions. But don't talk too long; there's a fine line between thoroughness and overkill. Two minutes should be the limit on the time you should take to answer any single question in detail.

Most good interviewers will wrap up by giving you an opportunity to ask questions. This is your opportunity to ask insightful questions about the company and the team that you may join. You want to take that opportunity to gain important information that you seek and to demonstrate your level of understanding and interest in the position. Appendix Q provides some guidance and a list of general questions.

You should conclude the interview with a verbal thank-you to the interviewer for their time and the valuable information they provided. But there is one last important thing for you to do before you leave: Ask for the job! Of course, you should make the request with finesse. We suggest ending your interview with a statement like: "I think I have the skills you are looking for, and I'd like to work for your company. What's the next step?" A question like this does two things. First, it lets the interviewer know that you want the job. Second, it prompts the interviewer to explain the decision-making process and timeline. You want to leave the interview with some expectation of when you will hear back from the employer. That may mean you will receive a call explaining that you were not selected for the job or that you were. You may receive a communication requesting that you return for a second or third interview. You need to have some idea of when it will be appropriate to follow-up about the position if you have not heard from the employer.

Always get the interviewer's business card or contact information. Follow up with an e-mail thanking him or her for spending time with you. In the message, reiterate your interest in the position. If you want to take it to the next level, write a handwritten thank-you letter and mail it by the next business day so that it is sitting on his or her desk two days later. You never know, the handwritten thank-you letter may make the difference between your selection and someone else's.

NEGOTIATING AN OFFER

Be prepared to negotiate before you arrive for your interview. If it is your first interview, then it is unlikely that you will receive an offer, but it is important to know your bottom line. Your bottom line is the minimum salary you would consider to accept an offer.

Salary negotiation is a bit of a game. Neither you nor the employer wants to be the first to suggest a number. The employer wants you to accept a salary in the lower range of a pay band that you will not know.

You want the highest salary that you can get. So, the first person to suggest a number anchors the negotiation around that number. Therefore, you want the employer to be the first to suggest a number. That way, you will know where you are in relation to your minimum salary requirement. You want the employer to suggest a salary that is above your minimum requirement, which probably means that there is some room to negotiate upwards to a higher salary. But, if an employer puts out a number that is lower than your minimum salary, you are going to have to negotiate just to get to your minimum.

Negotiation conversations typically begin with statements like: "What's it going to take to bring you onboard?" or "What salary do you feel you need to be at?" These are statements to get you to throw out a hard number. Your best response is "I'm sure any offer that you extend will be competitive with my knowledge, experience, and background." If you get into a position where you have to disclose a number, stay vague with a response such as "I need to be in the mid-70's." If you are working through a recruiter, they will already understand your salary requirements and handle the negotiation on your behalf. The recruiter will negotiate as high as possible, because recruiters are usually paid a percentage of the salary that they negotiate.

Be thankful and appreciative of any offer, but tell the employer that you will need to go home and think about it with your family and that you will give an answer by a specific time and date. Twenty-four hours is a reasonable response time that should be acceptable to an employer. This leaves the employer with the notion that you may be talking to other employers, which benefits you.

If you need to renegotiate, take the time to think about it and respond later via telephone and explain to them that you've been looking at things like cost of living and give them a hard number. For example: "I understand you have a salary cap, but if you can bring me on at $73,000, give me a three-month review, and if I've hit the milestones that you expect of me, I will be advanced to $77,000." You may also propose a sign-on bonus. Bonuses help a company maintain the salary structure while enticing you to come onboard. Most will have some discretionary funds to use as bonuses rather than spoil their salary band. Typical bonuses may run from $10,000 to $30,000 and so can get you close to where you want and still give you room for salary advancement.

Once you and the employer come to some agreement, you should get a formal letter stating your salary and other negotiated benefits. Read that letter carefully to make sure everything you discussed in your negotiation is included. If you accept the letter, you are ready to embark on the next phase of your career development.

CHAPTER DEBRIEF

- The secret to winning an interview is preparing well.
- Plan to arrive at the interview site 10 minutes prior to the scheduled time.
- Treat everyone that you encounter during the interview process as if they were the interviewer.
- Dress one level above the dress code, but be unremarkable in your appearance. You want the interviewer to notice your qualifications and your fitness for the job rather than how well or poorly you dress.
- Be prepared for anything. Interviews can take many different forms and require additional testing beyond the interview itself.
- Know yourself and your skills and experiences. Know your value proposition and your demonstrations of effectiveness. Practice answering potential interview questions but do not be shaken by questions that you did not anticipate.
- Use good judgment, but always ask for the job at the end of the interview and follow up by thanking the interviewer.
- Know your minimum salary expectation prior to an interview or a negotiation. Position yourself so that the employer is the first to suggest a salary. Don't accept the offer immediately. Ask for 24 hours to give the employer your final answer and potentially negotiate for a higher salary.

CHAPTER 10

DOWN RANGE: PUT YOUR CAREER PLAN INTO ACTION

Some of us know exactly what we want from an early age, and we go out and get it. Others have no clue and spend much or all their lives searching for their career. But, most of us, including these authors, lie somewhere in between. Jim found his career purpose many years ago and has executed his career plan with singular purpose. Will has reinvented himself on several occasions, and probably will again someday. To quote J. R. R. Tolkien, "Not all those who wander are lost," but successful people plan their future with clarity and purpose—and so should you.

We hope that, regardless of which end of the spectrum you find yourself, you will recognize the powerful career-planning model that we have introduced in the preceding chapters. We also hope that you have recognized the unique value that you bring to employers as a result of your military service. This book's central intent is to enable you to connect a structured career-planning process to your inherent skills and talents in order to fully develop a successful career of your choosing.

We have been asked, "What are hot careers for veterans?" The answer is easy—all of them. Your military service does not limit your options; it expands them. You have gained extraordinary leadership skills that are needed in every company. You have learned to organize things, people, and ways of solving problems. On average, your

147

communication skills exceed those of your civilian counterparts. You have gained knowledge through one of the most rigorous and comprehensive training and education systems in the world. You have put that training into practice in high-tempo military operations all over the globe and gained experience that is unmatched in any other endeavor. And you have the self-discipline to set goals and succeed.

That's your LOCKED value proposition. That's what's hot in the minds of employers.

RISING OPPORTUNITIES FOR VETERANS

If you are not certain what interests and industries might best serve you, we can suggest a few industries that are in dire need of your unique talents. Because we work in a multitude of industries, a few rising opportunities for veterans are out there—if your skill set and HDD match what an employer needs and offers.

Sectors that currently provide notable employment opportunities for veterans include high-risk industries like oil and gas production. In 2010 the BP Deepwater Horizon tragedy soaked the U.S. Gulf Coast in oil. That disaster has drawn very close attention to how oil and gas, and many other high-risk industries, operate safely. Those industries have come to realize that they could operate much more safely because the U.S. military operates in just as high-risk an environment as anyone, yet it operates with an extraordinary safety record.

No one could have made the point that high-risk military operations are a model for safety as well as Professor Nancy G. Leveson from MIT, who testified before the U.S. Senate in the wake of the Deepwater Horizon disaster. What she had to say is worth quoting at length. She said:

> We have never, for example, accidentally detonated a nuclear weapon in the 60 years they have been in existence.... No U.S. submarine has been lost in the 48 years since that program was created ... there is nothing very safe about flying in a metal tube 30,000 feet in the air in an unsurvivable outside environment, and kept aloft by two engines or being a mile below the surface of the ocean in a

submarine with a nuclear power plant. Yet these very dangerous industries are able to operate with very few or no accidents.[1]

The 2007 deployment of the U.S.S. *Enterprise* (CVN-65) was an extraordinary example of what Professor Leveson means. After the *Enterprise*'s nine-month deployment with nearly 5,000 sailors into two separate war zones where it launched more than 8,500 sorties, she returned home with no major injuries or incidents. Most aircraft carriers can boast similar results.

Whether you were a U.S. Navy nuclear power engineer or a U.S. Army Ranger, you understand the importance of safety and the need for mindfulness in a dangerous and often chaotic environment. Over the past few years, high-risk industries like oil and gas production have come to recognize the safety skills that veterans possess. Whether you seek a career in consulting, as we do, or working as a roughneck on an oil rig, there are opportunities out there for you. And even the roughneck jobs pay well!

There are aspects of the health care industry that also provide some great opportunities for veterans. If you are already in a military health care field or looking to pursue a post-military health care career, you have chosen well. There is much uncertainty regarding the ultimate impact of the Affordable Care Act (also known as Obamacare). What is certain so far is that there is a growing need for health care professionals both in the hospital and the home. As health care costs rise and the population ages, cost-cutting measures are forcing a reduction in the length of in-patient hospital care. Patients are forced to go home and rely upon much cheaper in-home care services. Whether it is as a nurse providing in-home care or as a manager that runs the many new businesses that are rising to meet this need, your skills are valuable.

Finally, and perhaps most importantly, veterans make great entrepreneurs, and America needs more of them. Veterans proved a natural talent for building their own businesses when they came home

---

[1]U.S. Senate Hearing 112-51: Oil and Gas Development before the Committee on Energy and Natural Resources May 17, 2011 (U.S. Government Printing Office) pg. 51.

from World War II. Today, veterans are showing that same talent by starting their own businesses and franchises. If you have a passion to blaze your own trail, utilize the same planning model that we have followed throughout this book to design the future of your own business, idea, or passion. History has shown that the skills you possess now have launched some of America's most successful companies.

Happy hunting.

APPENDIX A

THE SIX STEPS OF PLANNING

THE SIX STEPS TO PLANNING
1. Determine the mission objective.
   - Clear.
   - Measureable.
   - Achievable.
   - Support the high-definition destination (HDD).
2. Identify the threats.
   - Internal and external.
   - Controllable and uncontrollable.
3. Identify your resources.
   - Resources to achieve the objective.
   - Mitigate or eliminate controllable threats.
4. Evaluate lessons learned.
5. Develop a course of action.
   - Create a final course of action by determining *who does what, by when*.
   - Red Team the plan and incorporate Red Team comments into the plan.
6. Plan for contingencies.
   - Trigger/action matrix.

APPENDIX B

CAREER PLANNING WORKSHEET

PLANNING HORIZON:

HIGH-DEFINITION CAREER DESTINATION

INTERESTS: _____
_____
_____

ADVANCEMENT: _____
_____
_____

MONEY: _____
_____
_____

SECURITY: _____
_____
_____

PEOPLE: _____
_____
_____

CHALLENGE: _____
_____
_____

LOCATION: _____
_____
_____

TOP THREATS:

- _____
- _____
- _____
- _____
- _____

TOP AVAILABLE AND NEEDED RESOURCES:

- _____
- _____
- _____
- _____
- _____

TOP LESSONS LEARNED:

- _____
- _____
- _____
- _____
- _____
- _____

COURSE OF ACTION:

What   **When**

_____
_____
_____
_____
_____
_____
_____
_____

_____
_____
_____
_____
_____
_____
_____
_____
_____
_____
_____
_____
_____
_____
_____
_____
_____
_____
_____

CONTINGENCIES

Contingency	Trigger	Action

APPENDIX C

EXAMPLE CAREER PLAN

PLANNING HORIZON:

DECEMBER 31, 2022

HIGH-DEFINITION CAREER DESTINATION

INTERESTS: Employed by XYZ Corp. as an expert in learning and organizational development, leadership, coaching, and continuous improvement, with continuing opportunities for client interaction and the publication of written works (authorship).

ADVANCEMENT: Scope of impact and responsibility remains stable or increases respective to the overall growth of XYZ Corp. Opportunities exist for executive positions in the learning and development (L&D) field outside of XYZ Corp.

MONEY: $200K avg. per annum in total compensation with 4 percent company-matched 401(k) contributions; high flexibility in working hours and locations; multiple opportunities to continue personal and professional development that is mutually beneficial to employer and self.

SECURITY: Multiple options exist: remain with a growing and prosperous XYZ Corp.; obtain position in L&D with a mature and stable firm; undertake an entrepreneurial venture in private consultancy; assuming sufficient liquid capital, continue formal education in pursuit of a purely academic teaching career that leverages existing professional accomplishments.

PEOPLE: Continue to enjoy the family-oriented culture of a small firm like that of XYZ Corp.

CHALLENGE: Highly autonomous with considerable requirement for creative thinking and innovative productivity that is critical to the success of the organization.

LOCATION: Reside in current or similar home in North GA, with rural vacation residence in North GA or East NC mountains; option to work in home office; travel no greater than 25 percent.

TOP THREATS:

- Lack of professional certifications (e.g., CPLP).
- Lack of coaching and temperament assessment certifications.
- Two children college-age at planning horizon.
- Volatility of XYZ Corp. over span of planning horizon.
- Lack of professional learning and development mentor.

TOP AVAILABLE AND NEEDED RESOURCES:

- Strong virtual signature.
- Earned military retirement.
- TS/SCI that is current.
- Located in large urban market with many opportunities.
- Experience in multiple industries (service and light industries; training and education; continuous improvement).

TOP LESSONS LEARNED:

- Establish a greater professional and virtual signature by establishing a blog and being active on LinkedIn.
- Executive coaching is a career well suited to former military professionals and enhances the professional skill set of L&D and HR professionals.

COURSE OF ACTION:

What	When
Publish new manuscript	12/31/2013
Identify academic colleague for collaborative work	12/31/2013
Earn CPLP certification	6/30/2014
Identify CLO of large corporation as mentor	12/31/2014
Refine and compose manuscript for leader development program	12/31/2014
Earn executive coaching certification	6/30/2014
Identify two major clients for consulting work in L&D	12/31/2014
Seek elected office in local chapter of American Society of Training and Development (ASTD)	12/31/2015
Evaluate/Enroll in PhD program	12/31/2018
Identify North Georgia mountain property	12/31/2021

CONTINGENCIES

Contingency	Trigger	Action
Employment terminated	Two consecutive quarters negative growth	Engage network for options/opportunities

RESUME CONSTRUCTION TEMPLATE AND TIPS

Keep your resume clear and simple and presented in a logical format. Hiring managers often prefer to see your most recent experiences at the top and the dates of each employment experience. The first employment experience that a hiring manger will look at as they scan a stack of resumes is the first line that describes your most recent or current employment. If you don't get their attention on that line, you may lose them. Below is a basic template that will allow you to highlight your value. There are many different forms of resumes, and many different experts in resume writing that will prefer one form over another, but we recommend a chronological format. Seek the guidance of mentors in your particular career for advice and assistance in identifying the appropriate form and contents of a resume. (Note: If you are seeking employment with the federal government, the resume format that you should follow is very different from those of most other industries. Go to http://federalgovernmentjobs.us/federal-resume-writing.html for specific examples and assistance.

Your Name
1234 Address Line Rd.
Smallville, KS 09876
(123) 456-7890
Yname86@email.com

Experience

April 2011—Current	**Job Title**	**U.S. Army**

    Short Description of Job Responsibilities
    Demonstration of Effectiveness

June 2008—April 2011	**Job Title**	**U.S. Army**

    Short Description of Job Responsibilities
    Demonstration of Effectiveness

June 2006—June 2008	**Job Title**	**U.S. Army**

    Short Description of Job Responsibilities
    Demonstration of Effectiveness

Education

U.S. Army

Combat Lifesaver's Course
Expert Infantry Training
Preliminary Leadership Development
    Course (PLDC)

Smallville State College

Associate's Degree in Criminal Justice

RESUME TIPS

- **Do not capitalize all the letters in your name at the top of your resume.** An ATS may not read all caps well and reject your resume.
- **Do not use empty, trite, or insubstantial words and phrases in your resume.** Strive to craft a resume that is descriptive of your experiences and skills that are based in fact. Avoid using the following words and phrases unless they are part of a description that establishes a statement of fact, and that is

verifiable through hard evidence, recommendations, or awards. This list is for suggestion only and not entirely inclusive. It should provide some guidance regarding how to avoid wasting precious space on your resume.

Innovative: If you say you are innovative, you have to be prepared to prove it.

World-class: There's no generally accepted definition for this word, so it's best to avoid it.

Results-oriented: You will show results in your demonstrations of effectiveness (DOE); no need to say it.

Motivated: Don't say you are motivated; show that you are motivated through your actions before, during, and after an interview.

Creative: This is a very challenging adjective to prove unless you have substantive evidence.

Passionate: Like *motivated*, you have to demonstrate this through action; there's no point in saying it unless you can demonstrate it.

Incredible: Avoid using hyperbole in resume writing.

Team player: This is a given, especially for veterans, so there is no need to draw attention to what is obvious.

Strong work ethic: This is just a tired old phrase that has no meaning; don't use it.

Proven track record: If this is true, it will be obvious in the details of your resume.

Great communicator: This is a challenging description to prove.

Unique: Unique means that there is nothing else like it. Does that really describe your skills and experiences?

Dynamic: This is a word that sounds good, but few understand what it means.

Bottom-line focused: Great, you focus on the bottom line, but what about ethics and integrity?

Assisted in: This is a weak way to describe your contributions; avoid it.

- **Use a professional, unremarkable e-mail address in your contact information line.** If your e-mail address begins with something like HarleyMan or smokinweed68, then get a new e-mail account for professional correspondence. (Although, if you're applying for a job at Harley-Davidson, they might be impressed by HarleyMan.) A good e-mail address would be some configuration of your name, initials, and a number that doesn't have any questionable meaning.

- **Omit a "career objective" statement.** Statements outlining your career objective are most likely a waste of space on your resume. Omit them. State your objectives clearly in your cover letter.

- **Sell yourself on page one.** A resume may be one or two pages in length. However, it is vitally important that you target the contents of the first page to the opportunity you are seeking.

- **Avoid using fancy fonts and underlining.** Although they may be pretty and draw attention to specific skills and experiences, they can interfere with an ATS and, ultimately, cause you to go unnoticed!

- **Use proper punctuation and grammar.** Not only does such care indicate your ability to organize thoughts and written communications, improper punctuation has been reported to confuse ATSs, resulting in your resume being rejected before anyone sees it.

- **Never list references on your resume!** Make sure that the references you provide to a potential employer are aware of that particular opportunity, and are prepared to respond to a reference check. References should be briefed and engaged in getting you hired.

- **Answer every question on an online response.** Applicant tracking systems are generally programmed to reject applications with blank fields.

- **Do not send your resume as a PDF file.** Applicant tracking systems may not be able to read PDF text.

- **Use universally accepted fonts on your resume.** Pick a font that is easy for humans and ATSs to read. Times New Roman is a good option, as well as some sans serif fonts, including Calibri and Ariel.

APPENDIX E

COVER LETTER TEMPLATE AND TIPS

You should create a separate cover letter for each resume you send to a specific employer. Each letter should provide a concise introduction, mention your interests in the particular job, and highlight your relevant experience. Cover letters should not simply rehash your resume. While your resume provides details of your experiences, a cover letter explains why you are valuable to the specific employer. Below is a basic template for a cover letter. Refer to Chapter 8 for guidance on the second paragraph of this template.

Your Name
1234 Address Line Rd.
Smallville, KS 09876
(123) 456-7890
Yname86@email.com

December 27, 2013

Jane M. Boss (employer's name)
Director of Human Resources (employer's title)
ABC Corp. (name of company)
100 Corporate Blvd.
Metroville, KS 65432 (street address)

(continued)

Dear Ms. Boss,

Introductory Paragraph: Establish how you found out about the position. If you heard of the position through someone that you know who also knows the hiring manager, that is a great place to start. Establishing a common connection is powerful and memorable, giving you an edge. It compels the reader to reach out to that common connection and inquire about you.

Second Paragraph: Place your targeted value proposition here. What skills, talents, and experience could you bring to the position you're applying for? What about the company and industry are you especially excited about? Highlight anything about your experience, career goals, and professional personality that make you a great fit for the job and the employer.

Third Paragraph: Close your cover letter with a paragraph that states your interest and excitement about the potential to work in the advertised position and company. Conclude with a declaration that you would be excited to have the opportunity to meet to discuss your background. Finally, thank the reader for her time.

Sincerely,

Signature

GETTING NOTICED ON AN ATS QUERY

One of the great frustrations that job seekers encounter with larger employers is that their resumes are uploaded into an applicant tracking system (ATS) and stored in a database that is queried to match applicants to job postings. The end result is that the resumes of well-qualified applicants may never be seen by human eyes because the key word search program within the ATS did not identify a particular resume as matching the job posting. The secret to getting picked up in an ATS query is having a resume that contains the appropriate key words and phrases, so the ATS will identify a particular resume as a match to the job posting. If selected, a human being will then look over the resume and determine the qualifications and, potentially, contact the respondent for an interview.

It takes a bit of work and patience, but there is a way to beat the ATS and get noticed. Find several job postings that are similar to the kind of job you are trying to win on a web-based job postings site. Copy and paste the job descriptions and duties of those postings into a word-processing program and follow the steps and example that follows.

STEP 1

Copy several job descriptions of good opportunities within a specific narrow field into a word-processing program. The following list includes language from several different job postings, to give you a sense of what an ATS might be looking for:

This position is responsible for providing hands-on leadership in the design, development, implementation, and evaluation of the company's talent programs, including succession planning, performance management, development initiatives, change management, organization design and effectiveness, and employee engagement.

This position plays a key role in supporting the learning and organizational development function by developing and delivering solutions that drive organizational and individual performance to achieve key company strategies.

The effective candidate will interact with and support key business units across the company, and will build and maintain strong collaborative relationships with all areas of the company. Works with management on succession planning, leadership development, and effective utilization of talent to ensure an adequate talent pipeline.

Identify training and development opportunities to address individual business needs and gaps. Develop and implement a framework for leadership and functional competencies to include assessments.

Designs and develops training organization, management, and leadership development content to support learning and organizational development programs that promote and enhance overall individual and team performance.

Conduct and deliver leadership, management, and professional training. Evaluate and monitor the effectiveness of leadership training and development programs by analyzing data and providing feedback and/or modifications as needed.

Primary liaison with academic and professional organizations where needed to enhance the performance and talent management programs. Serves as organizational knowledge resource for change management. Develops and uses quantitative and qualitative methods and metrics to measure effectiveness of management and leadership development programs. Responsible for coordinating companywide engagement surveys and developing action plans and keeping departments accountable to those action plans.

Assist in developing companywide succession planning and leadership development. Oversee and administer the companywide recognition program.

Leads and actively participates in meetings and/or committees, as required. Performs additional duties as assigned. Delivers training via e-learning technology, classroom presentations, webinars, interactive approaches, social media, and interactive job aids.

Responsible for researching, developing, and implementing sales training and resources/tools that facilitate selling, in-servicing/presenting, negotiation, product evaluation and closing skills. Evaluates and recommends use of external sales tools and/or programs as appropriate. Determines learning effectiveness using follow-up and analysis of sales results, enhances as needed. Coordinates logistics and resources; conducts training sessions for individuals, groups, distributors, and division personnel; and coordinates field training activities of new and tenured territory sales managers and regional clinical specialists.

STEP 2

Carefully review the language you've collected in Step 1, then use bold to highlight what you consider to be the key words, as shown in the example here:

This position is responsible for providing hands-on **leadership** in the **design**, **development**, **implementation**, and **evaluation** of the company's **talent** programs, including **succession planning**, **performance management**, **development initiatives**, **change management**, **organization design** and effectiveness, and **employee engagement**.

This position plays a key role in supporting the **learning and organizational development** function by developing and delivering **solutions** that drive **organizational and individual performance** to achieve **key** company **strategies**.

The effective candidate will interact with and support key business units across the company, and will build and maintain strong **collaborative relationships** with all areas of the company. Works with management on **succession planning**, **leadership development**, and effective utilization of **talent** to ensure an adequate **talent pipeline**.

Identify **training and development** opportunities to address individual business needs and gaps. Develop and implement a **framework** for **leadership and functional competencies** to include **assessments**.

Designs and develops **training organization**, management, and **leadership development content** to support **learning and organizational development** programs that promote and enhance overall individual and team **performance**.

Conduct and deliver leadership, management, and **professional training**. **Evaluate** and **monitor** the effectiveness of **leadership training and development** programs by analyzing **data** and providing **feedback** and/or **modifications** as needed.

Primary **liaison** with **academic and professional organizations** where needed to enhance the performance and **talent management programs**. Serves as **organizational knowledge resource** for **change management**. Develops and uses **quantitative** and **qualitative** methods and **metrics** to measure effectiveness of **management** and **leadership development** programs. Responsible for coordinating companywide **engagement surveys** and developing **action plans** and keeping departments accountable to those action plans.

Assist in developing companywide **succession planning** and **leadership development**. Oversee and administer the companywide **recognition program**.

Leads and actively participates in meetings and/or committees, as required. Performs additional duties as assigned. **Delivers training** via **e-learning technology**, **classroom presentations**, **webinars**, **interactive approaches**, **social media**, and **interactive job aids**.

Responsible for researching, developing, and implementing **sales training** and resources/tools that facilitate selling, in-servicing/ presenting, negotiation, product evaluation and closing skills. Evaluates and recommends use of external sales tools and/or programs as appropriate. Determines **learning effectiveness** using follow-up and **analysis** of sales results, enhances as needed. Coordinates logistics and resources; conducts training sessions for individuals, groups, distributors, and division personnel; and coordinates field training activities of new and tenured territory sales managers and regional clinical specialists.

STEP 3

After you've determined which words to bold, delete the rest of the descriptions, leaving only the key phrases. This gives you a good overall sense of the types of things you should include in your resume. What follows is an example of what you will have left, using the text from Step 2:

leadership design development implementation evaluation talent succession planning performance management development initiatives change management organization design employee engagement learning organizational development solutions individual performance key strategies collaborative relationships succession planning leadership development talent talent pipeline training and development framework leadership and functional competencies assessments training organization leadership development content learning organizational development programs team performance professional training Evaluate leadership training and development data feedback modifications liaison academic talent management organizational knowledge resource change management quantitative qualitative metrics management leadership development engagement surveys action plans succession planning leadership development recognition program training e-learning technology classroom presentations webinars interactive approaches social media interactive job aids learning effectiveness analysis

STEP 4

Alphabetize the key words in a list, and then track the number of times that the word or phrase occurs. Use bold to help words that appear multiple times stand out. You will have a table like this:

academic	**leadership (2)**
action plan	**leadership development (4)**
analysis	leadership training
assessments	**learning (2)**
change	learning effectiveness
change management (2)	liaison
classroom presentations	**management (3)**
collaborative relationships	metrics
content	modifications
data	negotiation
design	**organizational (2)**
development (3)	organization design
e-learning technology	**organizational development (2)**
employee engagement	organizational knowledge
engagement survey	**performance (2)**
evaluate	programs
evaluation	planning
feedback	qualitative
framework	quantitative
functional competencies	recognition program
implementation	resource
individual performance	sales training
initiatives (2)	social media
interactive approaches	solutions
interactive job aids	succession
key strategies	**succession planning (2)**

talent (2)	training (3)
talent management	training and development
talent pipeline	webinar
team	

STEP 5

Now you have a list of words that are important to include in your resume—especially if you want to get through the ATS. At a minimum, use all of the bolded words and phrases in your resume, and include many of the other words and phrases as is appropriate given your experience and career HDD.

APPENDIX G

Practice Interview Questions Bank

THE STAR METHOD

The STAR method gets its name from the way you should formulate your answers to behavioral interview questions: situation, task, action taken, and result. It is a good means of organizing your thoughts, and it can help you plan for behavioral questions, which ask about how you have responded in particular situations in the past. STAR expands on the basic information that you will have crafted into your demonstrations of effectiveness (Chapter 8). STAR stands for the following structure:

Situation: Begin answering the question by citing the situation or challenge that your team or organization faces. Keep details to a minimum so you don't lose track of the big picture.

Task: Explain specifically what your task or mission was within the context of the overall situation. Consider framing it in the manner you would frame an intended effect or tactical objective.

Action taken: Explain what you did to accomplish your objective.

Result: Explain the result or outcome of your efforts. Make sure it's a positive outcome that demonstrates your abilities and value to the employer.

BEHAVIORAL PRACTICE QUESTIONS

What single project or task would you consider to be the most significant accomplishment in your career so far?

Describe a time when you were faced with a stressful situation that demonstrated your coping skills.

Give me a specific example of a time when you used good judgment and logic in solving a problem.

Give me an example of a time when you set a goal and were able to achieve it.

Give me a specific example of a time when you had to conform to a policy with which you did not agree.

PRACTICE QUESTIONS: BANK 1

1. Why do you believe you are qualified for this position?
2. Tell me about a time when someone on your team was struggling.
3. Do you consider yourself successful?
4. Give me a specific example of a time when you had to conform to a policy with which you did not agree.
5. Tell me about a time when you delegated a project effectively.
6. What qualities do you look for in a boss?
7. What irritates you about co-workers?
8. Are you more competitive or cooperative?
9. What would you do if you won the lottery?
10. What frustrates you in your current job/most recent job?

PRACTICE QUESTIONS: BANK 2

1. What is your greatest strength?
2. Why did you leave your last job?
3. Describe a situation in which you were able to use persuasion to successfully convince someone to see things your way.
4. Tell me about a time when you had to go above and beyond the call of duty in order to get a job done.

5. Describe a time when you anticipated potential problems and developed preventive measures.
6. Do you have any blind spots?
7. How long would you expect to work for us if hired?
8. Describe a situation in which you encountered cultural barriers that hindered your effectiveness.
9. Give an example of a time when you had strong convictions about a course of action but were subsequently convinced to use another approach.

PRACTICE QUESTIONS: BANK 3

1. Would you give a quick overview of your background?
2. What would your co-workers say about you?
3. Describe a time when you were faced with a stressful situation that demonstrated your coping skills.
4. Give me an example of a time when you had to make a split-second decision.
5. Tell me about a time when you were forced to make an unpopular decision.
6. Describe your management style.
7. Tell me about your dream job.
8. What are the three greatest risks you ever took?
9. Are your career plans more oriented toward technical or managerial positions?
10. What do you procrastinate over?

PRACTICE QUESTIONS: BANK 4

1. Why are you here?
2. Have you ever had to fire anyone?
3. Give me a specific example of a time when you set a goal and were able to achieve it.
4. Tell me about a difficult decision you've made in the last year.
5. Describe a time when you set your sights too high.
6. Tell me about a problem you had with a supervisor.
7. What was most/least rewarding about your previous position?

8. How do you organize your time?
9. What do you think you could contribute to this position and business team that differentiates you from others?
10. What are time wasters for you?

PRACTICE QUESTIONS: BANK 5

1. Tell me about a time when you had too much to do and too little time to do it.
2. Are you applying for other jobs?
3. Tell me about a time when you had to use your presentation skills to influence someone's opinion.
4. Give me an example of a time when you motivated others.
5. Describe your work ethic.
6. What would your previous supervisor say your strongest point is?
7. What is something you have done that made you laugh at yourself?
8. What kinds of books do you read? What are you reading now?
9. Describe a time when you discovered, or were told, about a deficiency in your job performance. What did you do?
10. Do you consider yourself successful?

TIPS FOR PRACTICE QUESTIONS: BANK 1

1. *Why do you believe you are qualified for this position?* Use your LOCKED value proposition.
2. *Tell me about a time when someone on your team was struggling.* Consider a positive leadership experience and use STAR to answer.
3. *Do you consider yourself successful?* The answer is "Yes," but you will have to explain why you consider yourself successful and explain briefly. Do not answer "No," because this demonstrates a lack of self-confidence.
4. *Give me a specific example of a time when you had to conform to a policy with which you did not agree.* Be careful! Use STAR to describe a time when you may have challenged a policy with respect and reason, yet carried out your duties in accordance with that policy. Demonstrate respect for authority and loyalty.

5. *Tell me about a time when you delegated a project effectively.*
   Use STAR. In business terms, a project could have been a
   mission you ordered a subordinate team to carry out.

6. *What qualities do you look for in a boss?* Be careful! Qualities such
   as a coach and mentor for your development and collaboration are usually safe. Consider the context before answering.
   Consider the qualities that you expect from yourself.

7. *What irritates you about co-workers?* Be careful! Saying "nothing"
   won't be believed. Choose minor, uncontroversial things like
   lack of communicativeness and how important it is for everyone
   to communicate openly to develop high-performing teams.

8. *Are you more competitive or cooperative?* Consider the context, but
   frame you answer in terms of "I am a bit more X than Y."

9. *What would you do if you won the lottery?* No one believes it if
   you say you'd keep your job, but you could say that you would
   engage yourself in activities much like the job you are applying
   for.

10. *What frustrates you about your current job/most recent job?* Be care-
    ful! You have to say something concrete, but keep it benign and
    uncritical of previous employers.

TIPS FOR PRACTICE QUESTIONS: BANK 2

1. *What is your greatest strength?* Consider one of your LOCKED
   values, such as leadership.

2. *Why did you leave your last job?* Consider your HDD and what
   circumstances led to your decision to leave the military. Portray
   your decision to leave in a positive manner.

3. *Describe a situation in which you were able to use persuasion to successfully convince someone to see things your way.* Use STAR. Be sure
   that you focus upon your ability to use reason and evidence
   to persuade while you are simultaneously sensitive to people's
   feelings.

4. *Tell me about a time when you had to go above and beyond the call of
   duty in order to get a job done.* Use STAR and one of your value
   propositions if appropriate. If you have a good military story to
   tell, go for it and stay positive.

5. *Describe a time when you anticipated potential problems and developed preventive measures*. Use STAR. You want to highlight a situation in which you demonstrated considerable analytical ability and expertise to save time, money, or even lives.

6. *Do you have any blind spots?* Consider carefully and choose something that doesn't expose a significant flaw. Its best to explain how you manage or overcome the issue you identify.

7. *How long would you expect to work for us if hired?* Be reasonable in your response. Employers don't want to get a sense that you are a temporary employee. But, if you say that you want to work for the company for 30 years, explain why you think so, and how it aligns with your HDD.

8. *Describe a situation in which you encountered cultural barriers that hindered your effectiveness*. Use STAR. This is a very important question if you are going to work in a global/international company. Craft a good answer that aligns with the context of the company!

9. *Give an example of a time when you had strong convictions about a course of action but were subsequently convinced to use another approach*. Use STAR. Everyone grows, develops, and makes mistakes. Tell a story of when you realized you were wrong and how you grew from the experience. But choose an experience that doesn't expose significant character flaws.

TIPS FOR PRACTICE QUESTIONS: BANK 3

1. *Would you give a quick overview of your background?* Use your LOCKED value proposition.

2. *What would your co-workers say about you?* Be positive, but humble. Be aware that a boss who is loved by their employees suggests that the boss is a pushover, while bosses that create fear and anxiety are poison to an organization.

3. *Describe a time when you were faced with a stressful situation that demonstrated your coping skills*. Use STAR. Consider a time (possibly combat) when you made a good decision with a positive outcome. Consider how it relates to discipline in your LOCKED value proposition.

4. *Give me an example of a time when you had to make a split-second decision.* Use STAR. This may be related to the question above, but it requires more focus upon your knowledge, experience, and your ability to prioritize.

5. *Tell me about a time when you were forced to make an unpopular decision.* Use STAR. You can use a situation in which you were ultimately wrong so long as you spin it as a growth and learning experience. Mention how you've incorporated what you learned into you leadership style.

6. *Describe your management style.* You probably want to twist this into a question about leadership style and explain the difference between management and leadership. You may want to highlight your organization and collaboration skills.

7. *Tell me about your dream job.* This is an HDD question. Be careful of how much the job you are interviewing for differs from that dream job. A good answer might relate to a different position in the company that you would develop into.

8. *What are the three greatest risks you ever took?* Overall, the message you want to send to the interviewer is that you are willing to take calculated risks, that you never bet the company, and that you are capable of managing risks through careful planning and contingency planning.

9. *Are your career plans more oriented toward technical or managerial positions?* Consider the context and be honest. It's usually best not to communicate a significant bias for one or the other, but rather to give a balanced preference.

10. *What do you procrastinate over?* Be careful! Stay away from issues that are directly work related.

TIPS FOR PRACTICE QUESTIONS: BANK 4

1. *Why are you here?* Use your LOCKED value proposition.

2. *Have you ever had to fire anyone?* Use STAR. This is a tough question, but one you must face. In the military you probably have had to pursue administrative discharges for punitive reasons. The message you want to communicate is that you have high standards and are not afraid to make difficult

decisions. Be careful to show that you make reasonable attempts to develop subordinates before terminating them.

3. *Give me a specific example of a time when you set a goal and were able to meet or achieve it.* Use STAR and answer with a LOCKED value proposition as the result.

4. *Tell me about a difficult decision you've made in the last year.* Use STAR to describe a situation that demonstrates your ability to deal with ambiguous or difficult situations and make the right decision for the organization as a whole.

5. *Describe a time when you set your sights too high.* Use STAR and spin this into a situation in which you bit off more than you could chew, but learned from the experience. It's best to keep this as a more personal anecdote than a business-related one. Be careful not to suggest that you are a big risk taker.

6. *Tell me about a problem you had with a supervisor.* Use STAR. This is a very dangerous question, but you have to answer it. It's best to explain a situation in which a supervisor was clearly wrong, but where you handled it with the tact and sensitivity to yield a positive outcome for all involved.

7. *What was most/least rewarding about your previous position?* It's easy to tell about the rewarding parts of your military service. Be careful with the least rewarding aspects. Don't answer with issues around separation from family because that does not answer the question. Consider your HDD and why you are pursuing it, then determine what part of your military service was at odds with that HDD. Stay positive.

8. *How do you organize your time?* Explain how well you plan and organize for each day.

9. *What do you think you could contribute to this position and business team that differentiates you from others?* Use your LOCKED value proposition within the context of the particular opportunity.

10. *What are time wasters for you?* Be careful. Meetings that don't drive specific action is a reasonably safe answer. Television and video games are a lame response.

TIPS FOR PRACTICE QUESTIONS: BANK 5

1. *Tell me about a time when you had too much to do and too little time to do it.* Use STAR. This is a question about task saturation, something we all face from time to time. Consider how you might prioritize objectives and seek support from your team.

2. *Are you applying for other jobs?* The answer is yes. You are always looking for opportunities to further your career HDD. Don't offer specifics. It is in your best interest for a potential employer to be anxious about the possibility of losing you to another employer.

3. *Tell me about a time when you had to use your presentation skills to influence someone's opinion.* Use STAR. This is a question that is testing your ability to present information in a rational, coherent, and convincing manner.

4. *Give me an example of a time when you motivated others.* Use STAR. This is clearly a leadership question. Consider utilizing your leadership value proposition.

5. *Describe your work ethic.* You are hardworking and believe that, when given a mission, it is your responsibility to ensure that mission is successful, regardless of the challenges and demands. As a leader in any organization, you believe that it is your responsibility to set a positive example for others to follow.

6. *What would your previous supervisor say your strongest point is?* Derive an answer that is reflected in your LOCKED value proposition.

7. *What have you done that made you laugh at yourself?* Use STAR. Be humble, but don't expose character flaws. Try to relay a benign situation that is from your personal life such as locking yourself out of the house. The message you want to convey to an interviewer is that you are not self-obsessed and unable to recognize and grow from your own folly.

8. *What kinds of books do you read? What are you reading now?* An interviewer, particularly an executive, wants to know that you are intellectually curious. You should always be reading a book

that helps you develop professionally and personally. If you don't read, start!

9. *Describe a time when you discovered, or were told, about a deficiency in your job performance.* What did you do? Use STAR. Tell a positive story that demonstrates a personal commitment to growth and development.

10. *Do you consider yourself successful?* The answer is yes.

APPENDIX H

INTERVIEW/OPPORTUNITY
PREPARATION CHECKLIST

PREPARATION FOR AN INTERVIEW

☐ Research the company.
- Go to the company's website.
  - Read the section labeled "About Us/Get to Know Us/ Careers."
  - Read recent press releases to learn about current events in the company and industry.
  - Review the remaining pages for greater situational awareness.
- Do a web search for relevant information/news/opinions about the company.
- Learn as much as you can about the company's culture, customers, and business offerings. The best way to learn this is by interviewing employees or others that are closely connected to the company or industry—perhaps even customers of that company.
  - Products and brands.
  - Top-selling products.
  - Relevant market and industry news.

185

- • Customers and target markets.
- • Competitors and how the company of interest distinguishes itself from them.

☐ Generate a list of thoughtful questions you might ask the interviewer.

☐ Practice answering potential interview questions prior to the interview.

☐ Find out the name(s) of your interviewer and how to pronounce it correctly.

☐ Obtain the specific address and other pertinent logistical information for the interview.
  - • If there's a specific interview location within a larger complex, how long is the walk from parking to the suite?
  - • Get the mailing address.
  - • If the interview will take place on a large corporate campus:
    - • Are there security check points? What are procedures?
    - • Where is parking and what building should you report to?

☐ Plan to arrive 10 minutes before the interview time. (Arrive no earlier than 15 minutes, and no later than 5.)
  - • Drive the route prior to the interview date if you live nearby, and plan accordingly.
  - • Make sure your car has sufficient fuel the preceding day.
  - • Make sure your car is clean with no visible clutter on the dash or seats.
  - • If you need to travel a long distance or by air, make a detailed travel plan in advance and anticipate traffic patterns.

☐ Get haircut or style if appropriate or needed. Your look should be conservative.

☐ Dress appropriately. (Refer to the attire checklists in Appendices I and J.)

☐ Clothing for the interview is cleaned and pressed.

☐ Wear only subtle fragrances, or none at all.

☐ Do not smoke prior to the interview.

☐ Determine how you will sit with appropriate posture beforehand without shifting and fidgeting.

MATERIALS FOR AN INTERVIEW

- ☐ A black or brown leather portfolio without logos. Inside be sure you have:
  - Pad of paper within with a clean top sheet.
  - Good quality pen (no logos).
  - Six hard copies of your resume and references list.
  - Any relevant paperwork that is required by the company (e.g., application, portfolio of work, writing sample).
  - Business cards, if appropriate.
  - Calendar, unless you use the calendar app on your phone.
  - Your list of questions to ask the interviewer. (Don't read from the list during the interview!)
- ☐ Carry an additional good-quality pen on your person or in a pocket.
- ☐ Cash for incidentals.
- ☐ Good-quality, undamaged umbrella if there is any possibility for rain.
- ☐ Needle and thread for last-minute repairs to clothing.

INTERVIEW

- ☐ Arrive 10 minutes prior to the interview but, if earlier, loiter near the interview location. Don't hang around the parking lot of the business.
- ☐ Park away from the main entrance, if possible.
- ☐ Do *not* chew gum.
- ☐ Turn your cell phone off or on a vibrate setting that can't be heard before going to the interview site.
- ☐ Treat everyone you encounter with respect, cheerfulness, enthusiasm, and politeness.
  - Don't be surprised if you are given tests to take prior to the interview.
  - Don't make phone calls in the waiting area.
  - Make polite conversation with others if appropriate, but don't be distracting or disruptive if others are working.

☐ Offer a firm handshake.

☐ Look around the office for some personal artifact belonging to the interviewer that may spark a common interest and politely ask about it to generate rapport-building conversation.

☐ Sit only if offered a seat.

☐ Ask for the job! *"I think I have the skills you are looking for and I'd like to work for your company. What's the next step?"*

☐ Thank the interviewer for his or her time, and when you might expect to receive some notice about a decision.

FOLLOW-UP

☐ Write a handwritten thank-you note within the next 24 hours and mail it to the interviewer.

- Thank the interviewer for his or her time and consideration.
- Make a comment on some topic that was discussed during your interview.
- Restate that you believe you are the right fit for the position.
- Summarize your value proposition in line with the needs of the employer.
- Explain, briefly, why you want to work for the company.

☐ If the promised follow-up date has passed, it's okay to ask about the status of a decision, so long as you are polite and phrase your question diplomatically. Doing so demonstrates interest.

ADDITIONAL TIPS

It's a numbers game. On average, 8 to 12 percent of interviewees for any given job posting are hired. That's just 1 in 10. That means that the average person must have at least 10 interviews to gain a single offer. The lesson for you is that you should not feel unsuccessful if you do not get an offer for every opportunity. Keep at it!

When in doubt, dress to the default standard. If you have clear direction on the dress code of a potential employer, dress one level above that required dress code. Keep in mind that one step above a business–causal dress code means that you dress in business attire, which is described in the default checklists in Appendices I and J.

Plan for potential delays. Consider the potential for having to clear a security check point in the building where you will interview. Leave extra time to pass security checks so that you are not late for an interview.

Create a written list of DOEs. Craft a one-page list of your most relevant demonstrations of effectiveness (DOEs) for a particular career opportunity and leave it with the interviewer after your interview.

Arrive 10 minutes before the interview. The optimal time to show up for an interview is 10 minutes. If you show up much earlier, you can impose on the interviewer's time. If you show up too close to the interview time, you may be perceived as having poor judgment. If you are late, you will have failed the interview in all but the most extraordinary circumstances.

Never say anything negative about a previous employer or employment experience during an interview. In general, interviewers will consider that you may be overly negative or critical and, therefore, not a good fit for their organization. Bottom line: Having negative comments about anyone or any company reflects poor judgment on your part.

Ask questions, but not obvious ones. Formulate intelligent questions for an interviewer that show you're well prepared, interested in the opportunity, and understand the company and industry. Do not ask questions that are easily answered by researching the company's website.

Follow up, but… Follow up with a company if they do not get back to you about a hiring decision in an agreed span of time. Do not hound a company for information. Excessive communication may be considered annoying, or evidence of a high-maintenance personality.

MEN'S INTERVIEW ATTIRE AND GROOMING CHECKLIST

The key to appropriate interview attire is to keep things simple. Do not wear anything that may distract the interviewer. Your appearance should be professional and tasteful, yet completely unremarkable.

Do:

- ☐ Make sure you're clean shaven.
- ☐ Keep shoes well-polished and clean (don't wear military/uniform shoes) with dark socks.
- ☐ Wear a belt that is in good shape and free of scratches.
- ☐ Invest in two suits. Keep the style conservative: dark color (e.g., dark grey, blue, or black), solid or with subdued patterns. Single- or double-breasted suits with two or three buttons are acceptable. (Two-button jackets are the current style.) Wool is always a good choice, but any high-quality fabric will do.
- ☐ Wear a high-quality white shirt with a straight collar.
- ☐ A good-quality tie with a conservative pattern in blue or red is always a good choice. Tie it with a double knot (when tied, the point should come down to about the top of the belt buckle).
- ☐ Ensure your dark socks will not allow any skin to be exposed when crossing your legs.
- ☐ Wear modest jewelry (no more than one ring per hand), if any.
- ☐ Wear a conservative wristwatch.

☐ Wear contact lenses rather than glasses. (If you must wear glasses, wear a conservative style.)

☐ Carry a handkerchief (not in your breast pocket).

☐ Keep your nails neatly trimmed.

☐ Be conservative with cologne (if you wear any at all).

DO NOT:

☐ Wear a lapel pin or miniature medals.

☐ Wear tie clip or pin.

☐ Wear a collar stay.

☐ Wear bracers/suspenders.

☐ Wear a vest (not even a matching vest that came with your suit).

☐ Wear cufflinks/French cuffs

☐ Wear military-issue shoes.

☐ Wear military-issue glasses.

APPENDIX J

WOMEN'S INTERVIEW ATTIRE AND GROOMING CHECKLIST

The key to appropriate interview attire is to keep things simple. Do not wear anything that may distract the interviewer. Your appearance should be professional and tasteful, yet completely unremarkable.

Do:

- ☐ Hair should be short or tied back.
- ☐ Invest in a solid-color, conservative suit with coordinated blouse in a pastel or other simple color. Wool or a wool blend is a good choice. A skirt or pantsuit is fine—choose something you're comfortable in. If you wear a skirt, it should be knee-length.
- ☐ Wear a good pair of polished dress shoes with a closed toe and back. They should have a two-inch heel at most.
- ☐ Wear a belt that is in good shape and free of scratches.
- ☐ Wear tan or light hosiery (pack an extra pair just in case you have a run or snag).
- ☐ Keep jewelry simple and classic; no dangly earrings or multiple necklaces or bracelets. Pick one statement piece of jewelry.
- ☐ Wear a conservative-style wristwatch.
- ☐ Wear contact lenses rather than glasses. If you only have eyeglasses, wear a conservative design.
- ☐ Keep makeup natural looking and conservative in application and color.

☐ Keep nails neatly trimmed and simple. Avoid wild nail polish or extremely long nails.

☐ Avoid bringing a purse or handbag; try to stick to carrying only a portfolio.

☐ Be conservative with perfume. Don't have an overwhelming scent.

Do Not:

☐ Wear a lapel pin or miniature medals.

☐ Wear military-issue shoes.

☐ Wear military-issue glasses.

SUMMARY OF VETERANS' CAREER AND TRANSITION RESOURCES

Relocation: Remember that at the end of your active service, the military will pay for you to relocate wherever you want within any of the 50 states or to your home of record. But you can only use this benefit once, so make a good decision!

Health care: Veterans are entitled to health care services through the VA Health System. However, health benefits vary widely depending on your condition of service. Go to http://www.va .gov/healthbenefits/apply to apply for VA benefits, or call 877-222-VETS (8387) *Tip:* If you become a drilling reservist, you are eligible for Tricare Reserve Select, which may be much cheaper than the health insurance provided by your civilian employer. Of course, Tricare is also available for retirees.

Education: The Montgomery GI Bill provides tuition assistance to both active and reserve veterans that qualify. There are a multitude of benefits that fall under the following acts: Post-9/11 GI Bill, Vocational Rehabilitation and Education (VR&E), Veterans' Educational Assistance Program (VEAP), Survivors' and Dependents' Educational Assistance (DEA), Montgomery GI Bill–Active Duty (MGIB-AD), Montgomery GI Bill–Selected Reserve (MGIB-SR), and Reserve Educational

Assistance Program (REAP). Again, the conditions of your service will dictate the exact benefits you may receive. You can go to http://www.gibill.va.gov to apply for benefits or find information about education benefits.

Home loans: Veterans are entitled to a VA home loan. In short, a VA loan allows you to finance the entire cost of the home. In other words, you do not have to make a down payment to buy a home. Most financial institutions (banks) will take care of all the paperwork for you if you choose to exercise your VA loan option. Depending on your financial situation, a VA loan may not be your best choice, so seek financial advice.

Life insurance: While on active or reserve duty you were entitled to Servicemembers' Group Life Insurance (SGLI). When you transfer off active duty or retire, you can convert that eligibility to Veterans' Group Life Insurance (VGLI). You will have to pay premiums based on your age and the level of benefits you desire. You can apply for VGLI online at http://www.insurance.va.gov/sglisite/vgli/vgli.htm.

Financial counseling: The VA provides financial counseling through FinancialPoint, a private company. You must be currently enrolled in one of the life insurance programs such as SGLI or VGLI to receive this benefit. You can go to http://benefits.va.gov/insurance/bfcs.asp for more information. Some financial services, such as USAA, may also provide free financial counseling, so check your bank and insurance companies for the services they provide.

Transition Assistance Program (TAP): At a minimum, each service provides a 3-day transition workshop to all transitioning veterans up to 180 days prior to their separation date. The U.S. Army provides a weeklong program as part of their Army Career and Alumni Program (ACAP).

Civil service employment preference: Many veterans (though not all) receive additional points toward a final score if they take a civil service exam in the process of seeking a job with the federal government. You may be entitled to as much as a 10-point preference, which adds ten points to your final score. To claim the preference, you must file form SF-15 before you take the exam. Veteran status does not guarantee a job with the federal government, just a preference through the point system. Find out more at http://www.opm.gov/policy-data-oversight/veterans-services/vet-guide.

LinkedIn Tips

- **Put your LinkedIn address in the signature block of your e-mail.** This lets potential employers know that you have a profile and provides them easy access to it. It also helps you build your LinkedIn connections by letting everyone know you have a profile.
- **Use your headline to declare your interest.** If you are actively seeking a new career opportunity, state "Seeking New Opportunity" in your headline.
- **Use a professional photo.** Post a professional headshot of yourself in interview-quality attire on your profile.
- **Use an unremarkable e-mail address.** Utilize a personal e-mail address that uses a combination of your name, initials, and numbers. Your e-mail shouldn't make a statement about your personality or interests. Your address should be like your interview attire—unremarkable.
- **Indicate results that you achieved.** Place your well-crafted demonstrations of effectiveness (DOEs) as a stand-alone statement beneath the description of each position you have held in your career in the "Experience" section of your profile. You do not need to have a DOE for every position.
- **Get recommendations.** Ask direct superiors for written recommendations to post on your profile so long as they are positive. Keep recommendations to just one or two for each position held.

- **Subscribe to LinkedIn Groups in your industry and profession.** Additionally, there are many military vet job-finding groups out there, such as Eagles Executive Transition Assistance Network, Military Leaders in Corporate America, Recruiters 4 Veterans, and U.S. Military Veterans Network. There are many more veteran-oriented groups as well as many professional and industry groups to choose from, and more are being formed every day.
- **Endorse others so that they are compelled to return the favor.** Currently, LinkedIn will automatically put potential recommendations at the top of your home page. As people endorse you, you see your top recognized skill sets appear at the bottom of your profile page—a pretty powerful graphic depiction of your primary skills!
- **Follow companies.** If there are specific companies that you are interested in, you can follow them on LinkedIn. So, sign up!
- **Use the InMail function to connect to recruiters.** LinkedIn boasts that recruiters are 30 times more likely to respond to an InMail than a cold call!
- **Do not blast all your contacts that you are in the job market.** Craft individual e-mails/InMails.
- **Use training videos.** If you opt to pay for the premium versions of LinkedIn, use the training webinars to leverage the full power of the tools.
- **CAUTION:** Be intentional in the information that you post on your profile. Everyone can see it and gain valuable intelligence from it.

APPENDIX M

LIST OF COMMON THREATS, RESOURCES, AND LESSONS LEARNED TO CONSIDER WHILE PLANNING YOUR CAREER

COMMON THREATS
1. You
2. Your virtual signature
3. OPSEC and recruiters
4. Flatness and civilian clothes
5. Language and general knowledge
6. Civilian misperceptions and stereotypes
7. Resumes
8. Applicant tracking system (ATS)
9. Interviews

COMMON RESOURCES
1. Standard veterans' benefits (Refer to Appendix K.)
2. Military leadership training
3. Reserve military service
4. Networking (LinkedIn and RallyPoint)
5. Mentors
6. Coaches
7. Recruiters

GENERAL LESSONS LEARNED

1. Research the company and the opportunity.
2. Consider timing, including the transition date and the standard hiring timelines.
3. Play the field, and seek multiple opportunities.
4. Establish career progression so your resume demonstrates a logical advancement sequence.

LIST OF ACTION VERBS FOR USE IN DEMONSTRATIONS OF EFFECTIVENESS

Each demonstration of effectiveness (DOE) should lead with action. Choose action verbs that are powerfully descriptive and vary between statements. In other words, don't compose 12 DOEs that begin with "Led …." Leadership is, indeed, one of your greatest values to an employer, but you have other skills. Below is a list of powerful action verbs you may consider using to start your DOEs.

Acted	Addressed
Administered	Analyzed
Arbitrated	Assessed
Built	Budgeted
Chaired	Coached
Coordinated	Created
Developed	Designed
Directed	Diagnosed
Engineered	Established
Executed	Improved
Increased	Integrated
Introduced	Led
Managed	Motivated
Organized	Originated

Operated	Oversaw
Performed	Planned
Produced	Shaped
Solved	Succeeded
Supervised	Transformed
United	Won

APPENDIX O

ADDITIONAL REFERENCES AND INFORMATION RESOURCES

There are so many information resources available to you that the variety itself is a threat. Where do you go to get good answers and directions? We have selected a few references and sources for you so you don't have to wander through the wilderness of information.

VETERAN SUPPORT AND BENEFITS WEBSITES

- Military One Source: www.militaryonesource.mil
  This is a great one-stop site for all things military. If you have a question, you can probably get some direction here.
- U.S. Department of Veterans Affairs (VA): www.va.gov
  If you have questions about your veteran benefits, this is the place to go. The website is easy to use and it provides a wealth of detail if you want it. If you have to fill out forms to get certain benefits, you'll find those here as well.

Skills Translation:

- O★NET: www.onetonline.org
  This site provides many career tools, but one of the most useful to you may be the crosswalk function that can help you translate your military skills into a language that employers can understand.

205

- Personal Branding Resume Engine: www.resumeengine.org
  This is a new site developed by the U.S. Chamber of Commerce. It is user friendly and can be helpful. However, we have tested it with a few common military skills sets to find it lacking. Still, it is new and under improvement. So, you should give it a shot.

Career Development Websites:

- Indeed: www.indeed.com
  Indeed is a global job search and posting site. You can search for jobs on this site, but the main purpose for including this site as a resource is the job trending information that you can find here. Indeed can help guide you to stable and growing industries and professions and even help you determine where to locate the best opportunity.
- Careerealism: www.careerealism.com
  It is very important that you keep up with trends in career management and development over the years. We have found this to be one of the best and most informative sites.
- Career Attraction: www.careerattraction.com
  This is another good site that puts out a lot of good advice.
- Contacts Count: www.contactscount.com
  Great site to help you develop your networking skills, something everyone can use.

BOOKS:

- *Flawless Execution: Use the Techniques and Systems of America's Fighter Pilots to Perform at Your Peak and Win the Battles of the Business World* by James D. Murphy
  We have only touched upon some of the basics of the Flawless Execution methodology. If you want to learn more and distinguish yourself in your new career with a powerful continuous improvement and learning model, read this.

- *Heroes Get Hired: How to Use Your Military Experience to Master the Interview* by Michelle Tillis Lederman
  This is a very in-depth but good resource to help you master the interview. The best part is that it's free! You can download this book at www.heroesgethired.com.
- *Combat Leader to Corporate Leader: 20 Lessons to Advance Your Civilian Career* by Chad Storlie
  For those of you with an army background, this book, written by a retired Special Forces lieutenant colonel, will help you translate what you already know into practice in your new career.
- *Please Understand Me II: Temperament, Character, Intelligence* by David Keirsey
  This is an essential guide to understanding how people differ in personality and provides guidance on how to communicate and interact with others. It also provides a good self-assessment survey to help you categorize yourself and understand your own temperament.

RECOMMENDED GENERAL BUSINESS BOOKS

If an interviewer asks, "What books are your reading?" you should answer with some title relevant to the profession or industry of the interviewer. There are many popular business books that are widely read that are good additions to the general business library. Here are a few:

- Jim Collins. *Good To Great: Why Some Companies Make the Leap … and Others Don't*. (HarperCollins, 2001)
  This is one of the most popular business books from one of the most influential business scholars of our time. It has even been widely read in military communities. It's a great place to start.
- Jim Collins and Morten T. Hansen. *Great By Choice: Uncertainty, Chaos, and Luck—Why Some Thrive Despite Them All*. (HarperCollins, 2011)
  This is Jim Collins's latest work and, in our opinion, his best.

- Joan Magretta. *Understanding Michael Porter: The Essential Guide to Competition and Strategy*. (Harvard Business Review Press, 2012) Michael Porter is the most recognized theoretician on business strategy alive today. However, his written work has a reputation for being dense and difficult to comprehend. This book, written by a close associate, is short, to the point, and comprehensible.
- John P. Kotter. *Leading Change*. (Harvard Business Press, 1996) Change management is an issue that most large businesses confront. Kotter is one of the most prominent scholars on managing change. He presents a simple change model in this classic.
- Patrick Lencioni. *The Five Dysfunctions of a Team: A Leadership Fable*. (Jossey-Bass, 2002) You are used to the "military way," but this book will demonstrate to you some of the common issues that you will face in civilian business—and how to overcome them. Lencioni is a best-selling author and this is one of his most widely read books.
- Connors, Smith, and Hickman. *The Oz Principle: Getting Results Through Individual and Organizational Accountability*. (Penguin, 2004) This is a bestseller about creating an accountable mindset in yourself and in the teams you lead. Your military background will serve you well in driving accountability—one of the great issues in business today.
- Chip and Dan Heath. *Made To Stick: Why Some Ideas Survive and Others Die*. (Random House, 2007) Another bestseller that is widely read by those in business development, sales, and marketing, but you'll find the contents applicable in many areas.

APPENDIX P

RECOMMENDED TASKS TO INCLUDE IN YOUR CAREER COURSE OF ACTION

WHAT (ACTION)	WHEN (DATE)
☐ Sign up for LinkedIn & RallyPoint profiles.	Today
☐ Identify at least five potential networking organizations.	Tomorrow
☐ Complete your LinkedIn & RallyPoint profiles.	Next 7 days
☐ Refine your demonstrations of effectiveness (DOEs).	Next 7 Days
☐ Refine your value proposition.	Next 7 Days
☐ Fully develop remaining individual strategic plans.	Next 14 days
☐ Join at least two professional/industry organizations.	Next 30 days
☐ Attend at least one networking event.	Every 30 days
☐ Answer/take notes on all five interview question banks.	Next 60 days
☐ Attend major conference of industry/professional organization.	Annually

TIPS FOR PREPARING QUESTIONS TO ASK AN INTERVIEWER

Asking good questions of the interviewer is essential to demonstrate your interest and engagement to a potential employer. Questions are also meant for you to gather additional information about the job and company to help you determine whether the position fits into your career plan and HDD. Here is some basic guidance for developing your questions:

- **Prepare a list of questions as you research the company.** Do not ask questions that could easily be answered online. You want the interviewer to respond, "Oh, that's a really great question!" when you ask it, and not be thinking, "Wow, this person really didn't do his research." The objective is to create insightful questions about what is going on with the company and its industry.
- **Prepare a list of questions that are important for you to understand about the job and the company.** Here are some examples:
  - What are the big issues on your horizon over the next year? Over the next 5 years?
  - What do you enjoy most about your (the interviewer) job?
  - What are the most essential skills and abilities required for this job?

- Why is this position open?
- What are the opportunities for employees to advance and develop?
- Do you have any concerns about my ability to be successful in this position?
- **Make notes and formulate questions during the interview.** The best questions will probably arise through the course of your interview. You should have a portfolio with you during the interview to take notes and jot down questions as they come up.

INDEX

McChrystal, Stanley, 23
McDonald, Robert, 19
McDonald's, 19, 67
Made to Stick (Chip Heath & Dan Heath), 208
Magretta, Joan, 208
Manager positions, 44–45
Matrixed ad hoc teams, 13
Medal citations, 127
Mentors, 95–97, 119
Military:
  employment vs. service in, 15–16
  hierarchical nature of, 12–14
  intrusive leadership in, 16–17
  mission-driven nature of, 14–15
  scale of, 11
  as temporary career, 87
"Military Experience & CEOs: Is There a Link?" (report), 22
Military One Source, 205
Millennials, 89
Minimum wage, 106
Mission-driven work, 14–15
Mission objective, *see* High-definition destination (HDD)
Money, 42–47
Montgomery GI Bill, 195
Murphy, James D., 206
Myers-Briggs Type Indicator, 69

NCOs (non-commissioned officers), 103
Negotiation, salary, 144–146
Networking, 43, 57, 90–94, 102
Nike, 32, 55
Non-commissioned officers (NCOs), 103
Notification of eligibility (NOE), 87

Objectives:
  within course of action, 116–118
  mission, *see* High-definition destination [HDD]
  on résumés, 164
Oil and gas companies, 148–149
O'Keefe, Brian, 29
O*NET, 205
Operational security (OPSEC), 70–72
Organization:
  defined, 25
  overview of, 26
  as principle, 10
  skills for, 128–129
The Oz Principle (Connors, Smith, & Hickman), 208

Pay band, 43, 46
People, in mission objective, 54–58
Performance, 91
Personal Branding Résumé Engine, 206
Personal information, 70–71
Personality tests, 56, 69, 141–142
Personality types, 56–57
Personal time off (PTO), 43
Petty Officer Selectee Leader Course (POSLC), 89
P&G (Procter & Gamble), 19
Philosophy, 54–58
Planning, contingency, 120. *See also* Career planning
Planning horizon, 33–35
Please Understand Me II (David Keirsey), 69, 207
Politics (of workplace), 93
Porter, Michael, 208
POSLC (Petty Officer Selectee Leader Course), 89
Post-traumatic stress (PTS), 75
Privacy, 10, 16–17, 69
Probationary periods, 16
Procter & Gamble (P&G), 19
Professional organizations, 74, 94
Profit-driven environments, 14–15
PTO (personal time off), 43
PTS (post-traumatic stress), 75

Qualifications, 81–82, 124

RallyPoint, 92
R&D (research and development), 50
REAP (Reserve Educational Assistance Program), 195–196
Recommendations, 199–200
Recruiters:
  and demonstrations of effectiveness, 125
  as resource, 97–98
  as threats, 70–72
Red Team, 119–120
Relocation services, 195
Research, on companies, 104–105, 135, 137–138, 185–186
Research and development (R&D), 50
Reserve Educational Assistance Program (REAP), 195–196
Resource(s), 85–100
  coaches as, 96–97
  common, 201
  dual career option as, 89–90
  impact of, 85